WORKOUTS
with WEIGHTS

SIMPLE ROUTINES YOU CAN DO AT HOME

**Stephenie Karony
& Anthony L. Ranken**

 Sterling Publishing Co., Inc. New York

To
Gloria Keeling

Acknowledgments

Thanks to Rick, David, Bill, and Clella,
our original Mastermind group

Photography by Steve Brinkman, Studio 44
Edited by Claire Bazinet

Library of Congress Cataloging-in-Publication Data

Karony, Stephenie.
    Workouts with weights : simple routines you can do at home /
Stephenie Karony and Anthony L. Ranken.
        p.   cm.
    Includes index.
    ISBN 0-8069-0325-2
    1. Weight training.   I. Ranken, Anthony L.   II. Title.
GV546.K37   1993
613.7′13—dc20   92-36155
                                                     CIP

10   9   8   7   6

Published in 1993 by Sterling Publishing Company, Inc.
387 Park Avenue South, New York, NY 10016
© 1993 by Stephenie Karony and Anthony L. Ranken
Distributed in Canada by Sterling Publishing
℅ Canadian Manda Group, P.O. Box 920, Station U
Toronto, Ontario, Canada M8Z 5P9
Distributed in Great Britain and Europe by Cassell PLC
Villiers House, 41/47 Strand, London WC2N 5JE, England
Distributed in Australia by Capricorn Link Ltd.
P.O. Box 665, Lane Cove, NSW 2066
Manufactured in the United States of America
All rights reserved

Sterling ISBN 0-8069-0325-2

Contents

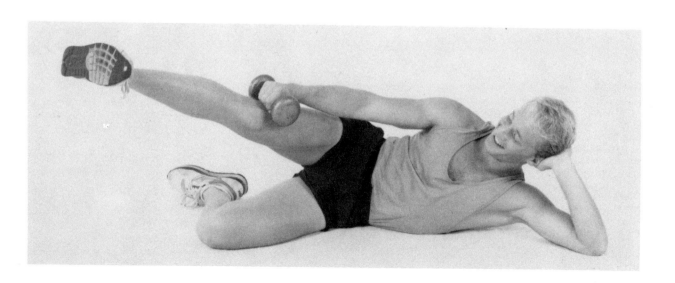

Introduction

Why Work Out with Weights?

Many people view strength training as a basically vain pursuit; that is, weightlifting makes your body more attractive. That's certainly true, but strength training is also an integral part of overall fitness. It is no accident that amateur and professional athletes in every sport now work out with weights.

There are five components of physical fitness: aerobic fitness, muscular strength, muscle endurance, flexibility, and body composition. Weight training enhances three of these five components.

Aerobic capacity refers to a person's cardiopulmonary condition; in other words, how efficiently and effectively one's heart and lungs deliver oxygen to the muscles. This type of fitness is achieved through exercise that elevates the heart rate for a prolonged period, such as running, cycling, and swimming. In order to obtain the benefits of aerobic training, you should exercise at 75 percent of your maximum heart rate, at least 3 times a week, for 20 minutes or more at a time.

Muscular strength is the amount of force that can be exerted by a muscle; in other words, how much weight you can push, pull, or lift. Muscular strength is the most obvious benefit of weight training. In fact, recent studies have demonstrated that, because of the beneficial effects of strength training on the nervous system, people who lift weights will experience some increase in strength in all parts of the body, even those areas that are not being directly exercised.

Muscular endurance refers to how many times the strength or force can be exerted over a period of time; that is, how many repetitions (or reps) of an exercise you can do. Muscular endurance is an important benefit of weightlifting and carries over into many daily activities. Simply put, you won't tire as quickly when doing physical work or play.

Flexibility is the measure of how limber your muscles are and how well your joints function. A flexible person has full range of motion in the joints.

Body composition is the ratio of body fat to lean body tissue, especially muscle. Weightlifting directly affects a person's muscle mass and/or muscle tone (muscular density), leading to a more desirable body composition. New evidence indicates that weight training may also help decrease body fat, a benefit long thought to be associated only with aerobic exercise.

These physical benefits of strength training can have far-reaching impact not only on your appearance, but also on your effectiveness and your enjoyment of life. Strong muscles support and protect the joints and make injuries less likely. Weight training strengthens the connective tissue (tendons) as well as the muscles. Weight training improves posture. It increases your energy and stamina. Agility and coordination are enhanced. Digestion and elimination improve. Blood circulation improves. Even the density of your bones is augmented by weight training, decreasing the risk of broken bones and helping to prevent osteoporosis.

Weight training can and should be done by adults of all ages; there is no upper age limit. Strengthening your muscles, bones, and joints with the programs in this book will guard against many of the undesirable changes associated with aging. As long as you keep up a moderate program of strength training (even twenty minutes three or four times a week), you will not experience the weakness that restricts the lives and movement of many old people, causes loss of balance accompanied by increased falls and broken bones, and prevents them from taking care of their daily needs and living independently. For young and old alike, strength training helps prevent debilitating injuries in all pursuits; being stronger, you are less likely to fall or have accidents while engaging in sports or everyday activities. If you do fall, the stronger bones, muscles, and tendons produced by weight training will decrease the likelihood of injury.

Studies show that for every decade after the age of twenty the average person's metabolism slows down by approximately four percent in the absence of exercise. You also lose about one percent of your lean muscle tissue every four years after age twenty, if you're not exercising. Weight training, especially when combined with an aerobic exercise program, can slow down and even reverse these losses.

On the mental and emotional level, the benefits of weight training can also be very significant. Weightlifting helps strengthen self-discipline. You're doing something that's not easy, on your own, and this discipline in one area carries over to other areas of your life. Concentration is also improved, as is alertness; the exercises in this book require you to focus on and think about what you're doing. For reasons that may be physiological as well as psychological, most people experience a significant increase in self-confidence, a feeling of "empowerment," when they begin lifting weights. Your self-image improves because your body looks better. This leads to better attitudes about yourself and life. Last, but certainly not least, a good workout is a great stress reducer. In general, and for whatever reasons, people who are committed to a weight-training program report that they feel better on all levels.

Even though we talk about the physical, mental, and emotional aspects of our being separately, they are in reality not separable. Being physically fit and having a strong body inevitably improves your psychological well-being. Mental and emotional health, in turn, enhance your physical health and well-being.

Working Out with Dumbbells

There are several ways to approach strength training: health clubs with state-of-the-art machines and racks of free weights (barbells and dumbbells), fancy home gyms and machines costing hundreds to thousands of dollars, and gadgets for working particular body parts. The most versatile system of all is also the most convenient and least expensive: a simple set of dumbbells.

This book will show you how dumbbells can give your entire body a high-powered workout just as effectively as any bulky home gym or expensive specialized machine. In fact, dumbbells have some important advantages over other

A pair of hand-held dumbbells is all you need for an effective full-body workout.

strength-training equipment. They are inexpensive and easy to store, and will last a lifetime without ever breaking down or requiring maintenance. Dumbbells give you flexibility; you can use them anytime, anywhere, and even take them travelling. (Think of the bonus workout you'll get lugging them to your car or the airport in a suitcase!) Compared to home machinery, dumbbells are far more versatile; they permit you to exercise every part of each muscle. And compared to a gym, health club, or spa, a home dumbbell workout saves not just money but driving time. If you're a working person with a busy schedule, or a parent with children at home, that could make the difference between sticking to your exercise program or not!

In addition, a dumbbell workout is more effective and produces quicker results than using machines. The movements involved in lifting dumbbells are closer to real-life movement, so they help strengthen your muscles for practical purposes. For this reason, if you're interested in improving your performance in any sport, free weights are a better choice than machines.

With free weights, you work more muscles with each exercise. While a machine isolates one particular muscle, dumbbells exercise the assisting and stabilizing muscles as well. (For example, a Shoulder Press with dumbbells also strengthens your triceps and biceps.) For the same reason, dumbbells are most effective in improving your coordination and balance, and a free-weight workout is the best way to give your body proportion and symmetry.

If you have a complete home gym set or a barbell and weight bench, you may wish to supplement your workout with a few exercises using that equipment. Barbells and home gym equipment are useful (but not necessary) for chest and back exercises. For a number of the exercises in this book, you will find "variations" to be done with a barbell or other gym equipment. We have also included a few exercises and programs specifically for use with this equipment, as a supplement to the basic dumbbell workout.

Weight training, once the province of a small segment of the male population, is being discovered by more and more men and women from all walks of life, who are finding in this form of exercise an efficient and effective way to improve not only the appearance and health of their bodies, but also the overall quality of their lives. Our goal in writing this book is to make strength training simpler and more convenient than ever. We will show you how to get a full-body workout with nothing but a set of dumbbells and this guide, and you can do it in the quiet of your own home or while listening to your favorite music. Enjoy!

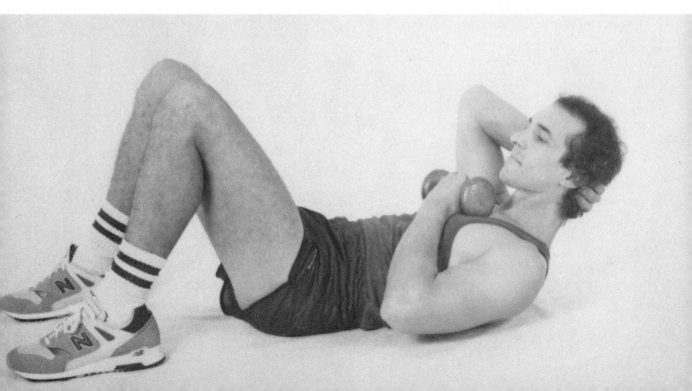

CHAPTER ONE

Getting Started

About Dumbbells

There are several kinds of dumbbells available. Any of them will work fine for the exercises in this book. The most popular and durable dumbbells fall into two categories: solid-cast dumbbells and dumbbells with removable plates.

Solid-cast metal dumbbells, some of which are chrome-plated, come in a fixed weight. If you choose solid-cast dumbbells, you will need to purchase two to four pairs of progressively heavier weights. This is because some of your muscles are naturally stronger than others, and also because you will be increasing the amount of weight used in each exercise as you get stronger.

Removable-plate dumbbells will be less expensive if you are using several different weights. However, they are also less convenient because you will have to remove and replace plates to

The most inexpensive and versatile home workout equipment—dumbbells and push-up bars.

adjust the weight, instead of just picking up a different set of dumbbells. Some exercises are more difficult if the loading bar of the dumbbell is long; choose a set with a relatively short bar from end to end.

Solid-cast dumbbells generally cost between one and two dollars per pound. Removable-plate dumbbells range from $25 to $100 a set, depending on the quality and total weight.

Solid-cast dumbbells are hard to find in weights higher than 25 pounds. They are generally more suitable for women, who rarely exceed this limit. Men can start with solid-cast dumbbells but may have to switch to the removable-plate type for some of the exercises, as they become stronger.

To keep dumbbells clean and rust-free, rub oil on them once or twice a year, especially if you live in a damp climate. That is the only maintenance they will need to last a lifetime.

Before You Start

There are several things you should do before you start working out with weights:

Physical Exam   It's best to have a physical exam and get your doctor's okay. This is especially true for anyone who has a personal or family history of heart trouble or who has been relatively sedentary.

If you have doubts about whether you are physically prepared to start an exercise program such as this, then take it slowly. Start with light weights, and gradually work your way up to more challenging workouts. Listen to your body.

Taking measurements will help you chart your progress and keep you motivated.

Set Some Goals Decide what you want to gain from working with weights. Do you want to get stronger? Tone and shape your body? Develop bigger muscles? What areas of your body do you want to emphasize? Your workouts will differ depending on your goals. (See page 148, for how to tailor your workouts to your personal goals.)

Don't expect results overnight. You will see progress soon enough. Set yourself smaller, reachable goals at first, like working out for 45 minutes 3 times a week. One great way to notice your improvement and keep yourself motivated is to keep a record of your workouts. Also, you might want to record your body weight and key measurements: upper arm, upper and lower chest (men) or bust (women), waist, upper hips including lower abdomen, lower hips including buttocks, mid-thigh, knee, mid-calf, and ankle.

Find the Time (and Place) to Exercise Anytime is the right time for weight training; it's a matter of fitting it into your daily schedule. Choose a time for your workout when you will have as few

Warm up by moving your body . . .

10

. . . in whatever way you like.

distractions as possible. After a while you may notice that your workouts go better at certain times of day; try to plan your workouts for times when your energy level is high.

Gather your dumbbells and all of the equipment you will need (a chair, stool, or whatever the particular exercises call for that day). The room should be large enough to allow you to move about freely. It should have a mirror if possible, and good air circulation.

What to Wear   Dress to move. Wear something that won't restrict the movement of your body in any way. Avoid seams or zippers up the back (they will be uncomfortable when you lie down for abdominal work). Use athletic shoes that provide some support for your arches. If you're exercising in a cold climate, wear a warm-up suit or sweats to keep your muscles warm and prevent injury. Avoid rubber or vinyl exercise suits; always wear clothing that absorbs perspiration and allows your body to "breathe."

Warming Up   A good warm-up prepares the body for movement. Warming up increases the blood flow to your joints and muscles, which enhances their performance and helps to guard against injury. In short, warming up prepares your body for the stress of lifting weights.

Good ways to warm up your body generally are to jog in place, do jumping jacks, ride a stationary bicycle, or do some sit-ups before lifting weights. Chapter 5 contains some good warm-up exercises for the specific parts of your body that you plan to exercise.

As you progress to heavier weights, it is also important to do a light set for the first set with each body part (about a third to half of your normal weight for that exercise).

NOTE: Contrary to popular belief, stretching is an ineffective way to warm up. Like any other form of exercise, the benefits of stretching are long term. Stretching prepares you to do other physical activity such as weightlifting safely, but that does not mean you need to stretch right before lifting weights; we prefer to do it after our workouts. You can stretch before your workout if you like, but be sure to do some warm-up exercises first.

CHAPTER TWO

Basic Principles of Working Out

Reps and Sets

"Rep" is short for repetition; that is, one weight-lifting movement. A "set" is a group of reps done without pausing in-between. Any number of sets and reps will do your muscles some good, but for the most efficient and effective workout you should do *3 to 4 sets* of *8 to 12 reps per set*. When you are able to do 12 reps of a given exercise, it is time to increase your weight on that exercise.

The size of dumbbell you use depends on your goals as well as your strength.

NOTE: The floor exercises for legs, buttocks, and abdominal muscles are an exception to this rule. In the descriptions of those exercises you will see that higher numbers of reps are prescribed.

If you are interested in building muscle mass, do fewer reps (5 to 8) at a heavier weight. If all you are after is muscle tone and endurance, you may do 12 to 15 reps per set at a slightly lighter weight. However, the basic formula of 8 to 12 reps provides a quality workout for both men and women who want to get the maximum overall-fitness benefit from weight training.

Rest after each set. The rest should be long enough so that you can finish your next set. There is no fixed rest time; it differs according to your constitution, how much weight you are lifting, which body parts you are working, and how you are feeling on a given day. By the process of trial and error you will soon learn how long to rest between sets.

Correct Order of Exercises

Start with the exercises for the larger muscle groups (thighs, back, chest) and work your way down to those for the smaller muscles (shoulders, triceps, biceps, calves, forearms). The workout programs in chapter 8 take care of this for you. If, as you gain experience, you wish to design your own workouts, this order of exercises is the most important principle to keep in mind.

"Working the Negative"

The "negative" motion is the return of the weight to its original position. Although you are lowering the dumbbell during this part of the movement, it is an equally important part of weight training, both from a standpoint of muscle development and injury prevention. You should let the weight down at the same rate as you lift it or even a little slower. Injuries most often occur during the negative motion, because this movement puts greater stress on the tendons. Besides, you will find that the negative motion is just as difficult as the lifting movement and therefore is of great benefit to the muscles; if you lower the weight too fast you are letting gravity do the work and depriving yourself of the full benefit of the exercises.

Balance

There's nothing wrong with emphasizing one area of your body in your workouts. Chapter 8 provides several balanced workout programs emphasizing the upper or lower body. If you create your own programs, be aware of the principle of *balance*: every major muscle in the body has an opposing muscle (such as, triceps/biceps, chest/back, quadriceps/hamstrings). It is important not to emphasize one muscle at the expense of the other. An imbalance caused by training biceps much more than triceps, for example, could cause a triceps injury, as well as put undue stress on the joints. Aside from these health concerns, an evenly developed, well-proportioned body is more attractive.

Stretching

Why stretch? It helps achieve and maintain flexibility in the muscles and a full range of motion in the joints. Flexibility is one of the five components of fitness, discussed in the introduction to this book. In addition, stretching reduces muscle soreness that may result from any form of exercise. Because of the importance of stretching, we have included a whole chapter on it. See chapter

Stretching has psychological as well as physical benefits.

6 for the correct way to stretch, when to stretch, and instructions on stretches for each part of your body.

Keep a Workout Log

Set aside a notebook just for your training sessions. Record the date, time of day, the number and level of the program (if you're using one of the programs in chapter 8), and for each exercise list the number of sets, the number of reps per set, and the amount of weight used. You may want to note anything that might have a positive or negative effect on your workout that day, such as being short on sleep, your energy level, stress level, if you drank alcohol the night before, or if you blew your diet. Finally, if you're trying to lose or gain weight, leave a space on the log to record your weight once a week or so, and your measurements every month or two.

A workout log can help keep you on track.

By reviewing your workout log periodically, you will notice areas of fast improvement and also weak spots. You will find that seeing the improvement is a great motivator. If you are not improving in certain areas, it is a sign that you need to focus on those body parts.

Stick to Your Program

Why stick to your program? Because consistency is what will produce results! Don't be affected by what friends or other books have to say. There are many different philosophies on strength training and weightlifting. The programs in this book are designed for effective, whole-body training, with safety a primary consideration.

Each week, set yourself a training schedule and stick to it the way you would to your work or social calendar. Even if you're tired, force yourself to go through with it. Often you will find that your energy picks up after a few exercises. If you have to miss a workout now and then, don't be too hard on yourself. Reschedule it if you can. As long as you consistently work out a minimum of three times a week, you will continue to see results. On the other hand, don't exceed the number of workouts recommended in the programs in chapter 8. In weight training, more is not necessarily better; too-frequent workouts may result in overtraining, which can make you more susceptible to injuries and undo the progress you've made.

One great way to get yourself to stick to a program is to work out with a partner. You won't make excuses to a friend as readily as you would to yourself. Also, you'll probably find that you and your workout partner motivate each other; you'll likely have more energetic workouts and progress more rapidly.

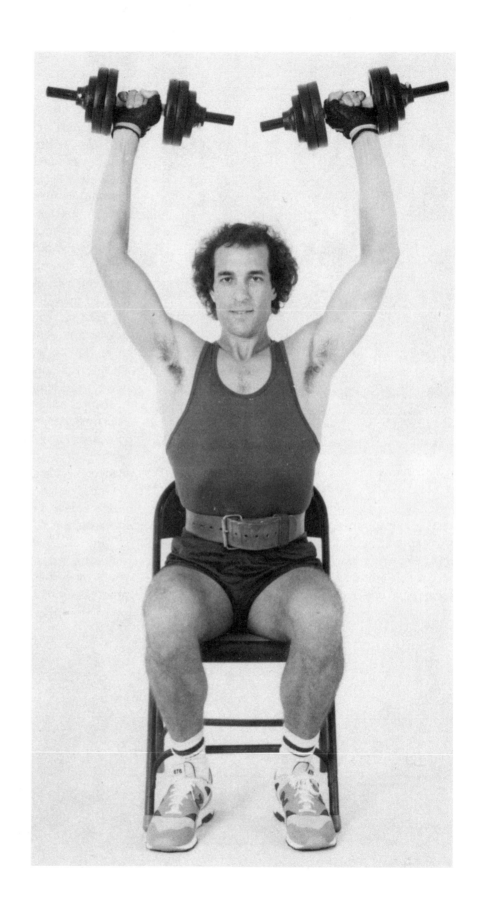

CHAPTER THREE

Understanding and Enhancing Your Training

What Determines Muscle Development

There are a number of factors that determine how fast a person can progress on a strength-training, muscle-toning, or bodybuilding program. Some of these factors are beyond your control, while others are personal choices within your control. Of the factors which you must take as given, the biggest variable is your sex; men develop larger muscles when they lift weights, while women on the same weightlifting program will develop firmer, shapelier bodies but will add little muscle size. Another major factor is age; although adults of any age can undertake a successful weight-training program, progress happens faster when you're younger. Whether you were active in younger years also counts; those who have exercised regularly since childhood or who were athletes in high school or college can build muscles and strength faster. Finally, genetics plays a role as well; some people's muscles are better adapted to short bursts of physical activity, while other people shine at endurance exercise. No matter where you fall on the spectrum, you can gain great benefits from weight training.

Don't be discouraged at this point — no matter what your age, sex, or exercise history, your strength-training success is largely within your control. A wholesome nutritious diet is a big factor. The basic principle to keep in mind for an ideal diet is to get the most nutrition possible from the least amount of calories; for example, the one hundred calories contained in a piece of fresh fruit will do your body much more good than the one hundred calories you get from a small piece of chocolate cake.

Your performance and progress will also be enhanced if you get plenty of sleep. Another question is how often (and how much) you drink alcohol, smoke, or take recreational or mood-altering drugs. If you don't want to eliminate these things entirely, at least keep in mind that moderation will improve your workouts and your health. Last but certainly not least, your progress depends on your attitude and commitment: your attitude toward yourself, your health, and your fitness, and your commitment to exercising regularly and energetically. (And remember, you can't expect yourself to exercise energetically unless you're eating correctly and getting enough rest!)

Joint Conditioning

Virtually all modern athletes use weights in their sports training programs. The reasons are twofold. The most apparent is that the muscles grow stronger. Another important reason is that the connective tissue also grows stronger. The connective tissues most affected by weight training are the tendons (which hold muscle and bone together) and perhaps to some small degree the ligaments (which connect two or more bones and are responsible for the stability of the joint).

If you are just beginning a weight-training program or have not lifted weights recently and regularly, avoid the temptation to try lifting heavy weights at first. You must consider not only your muscular strength (how much you can lift), but also your joint strength (how much resistance the connective tissue can handle). A joint injury can be much more serious than a muscle injury. To make sure you don't injure your joints, start with light dumbbells for the first few weeks, and add weight slowly, even if your ultimate goal is to add strength and size. Be sure to perform at least one of the stretches described in chapter 6 for each body part you work; stretching works on the flexibility of the joint as well as of the muscle. Lift the weight through the joint's full range of motion as instructed in each exercise; doing abbreviated movements puts undue stress on the joint. Be very careful not to jerk the dumbbells; strive instead for a slow, controlled movement. Finally, listen to your body. Sore muscles are usually just a sign that you've had an effective workout, but pain in the joints is not normal. If your joints hurt after a workout, lighten your load!

To make sure you are working out correctly and guarding against injury, take the time to read (and periodically re-read) the safety rules and the injury prevention guidelines (pages 21–23).

Diet and Nutrition

A good, nutritious diet is a key element of a healthy lifestyle and an effective weight-training program. Foods are categorized by the nutrients they contain; to ensure a nutritionally complete diet, choose foods from each of the following food groups:

1. Grains and cereals
2. Vegetables
3. Fruit
4. Meat, fish, poultry, eggs, beans, legumes, nuts and seeds
5. Dairy products, such as milk, cheese, yogurt (preferably lowfat or nonfat)

Look at the overall structure of your diet over a period of days; don't worry too much about your intake on any particular day. Try to average more servings per day of grains and cereals, fol-lowed by vegetables and fruits, than servings from the other food groups.

Every food contains some or all of the six basic nutrients needed by your body. Wholesome eating requires a basic knowledge of these nutrients:

Carbohydrates are your body's most efficient and best source of energy. Good sources of carbohydrates are groups 1, 2, and 3 above (grains, vegetables and fruits).

Protein builds and repairs your muscles and other body tissues. The best sources are food groups 4 and 5. Grains and vegetables also contain some protein, but if you depend on non-animal sources for your protein needs, be sure to eat a variety of protein-rich foods in order to get all the different amino acids you need. (The best book on protein for vegetarians is Frances Moore Lappe's *Diet for a Small Planet* [twentieth edition, 1991].) Because of the importance of protein in muscle development, don't shortchange yourself in this category, but do get as much as possible of your protein from low-fat sources such as egg whites, fish, chicken, skim milk, nonfat yogurt, beans, and legumes.

Vitamins are found in all foods. They help regulate the metabolism and protect the body from disease.

Minerals activate your body's enzymes, which are necessary for metabolism. All foods contain minerals; the richest sources are organ meats, beans, peas, and green vegetables. Minerals are especially important for those on any exercise program because they maintain the body's electrolyte balance. Avoid too much sodium (salt); excess sodium can contribute to water retention and high blood pressure. With a balanced diet, table salt isn't necessary; sodium is found naturally in most foods.

Water, found in fruits, vegetables, and liquids, is the most essential nutrient of all; you can't survive more than a few days without it. It transports nutrients, regulates body heat, and aids in digestion.

Fat protects your organs, insulates your body, helps assimilate certain vitamins, and stores energy. Although some fat in your diet is essential, don't use that as an excuse for unwholesome eating; most of us eat far more fat than we need, and fat contains more than twice as many calories per gram as carbohydrates. As long as you're toning and shaping your muscles, you don't want to hide them under layers of fat! (Not to mention the increased risk of heart disease associated with a diet high in fat.) Sources of fat include meat, shellfish, dairy products, vegetable oils, and nuts. Even grains contain small amounts of fat. Unsaturated fats (most vegetable sources) are healthier than saturated fats (meat, dairy, and the tropical oils—coconut and palm oil). One of the easiest ways to reduce your fat intake is to opt for nonfat or skim-milk products. The protein, vitamin, and mineral levels are not affected but the amount of fat is greatly reduced.

If you would like to drop a few (or more) pounds while you're toning your muscles, our best advice is to combine the exercises in this book with an aerobic exercise program (which burns more calories) and sensible, moderate eating habits. Avoid drastic or fad diets that starve you and deplete your energy. Such diets will make it more difficult to stick to your exercise program, and they do not change your long-term eating patterns. Once you quit the diet, you'll revert to your old eating habits and gain back whatever weight you lost. Instead, just get plenty of exercise, reduce your caloric intake, and try to incorporate a basic awareness of smart versus foolish food choices. As you become more attuned to your body's needs, you'll find that it affects your tastes. A piece of fruit will make a more pleasing snack than a candy bar, and you'll realize that you don't really want that cheesecake or that second helping of pasta.

Visualization

Believing something will happen directs the subconscious mind toward choices that will help make that thought a reality. The subconscious is your ally and can be a powerful force in achieving your goals. Visualization is consciously programming your subconscious. Through visualization, you can tell your subconscious mind to stay on your diet, to train each day according to the goals

More and more people are recognizing the benefits of visualization.

you've set, and to stay motivated. You can visualize how you would like to look, make this image real in your own mind, then proceed to do what's necessary to manifest the image in your life.

Here is a simple visualization process: Sit quietly with your eyes closed, either cross-legged on the floor or in a chair with your back supported and your feet flat on the floor. Give yourself a minute or two to relax. One effective way to relax is to focus on relaxing each part of your body in turn, starting from your face and gradually working down to your feet. Another way is to breathe deeply and steadily, focusing your attention on your breath as it flows in and out. When you feel relaxed, allow an image to come into your mind's eye of yourself, your body, or your behavior as you would like yourself to be. Make the picture as clear as you can, filling in all the details you can think of. Think of it not as a future ideal but as a present reality. If you like, while holding the image in your mind, you can silently repeat to yourself affirmations, phrased in the present tense, expressing your ideals — "I am slender and strong," "I have control over how I look," or "I eat foods that nourish and strengthen my body." Invent your own affirmations, ones that feel right for you. Stay with your images for as long as you like, then take some deep breaths and gradually open your eyes. Carry your images with you in your daily life. As you're doing the exercises in this book, you might want to conjure up the body image you've visualized, or as you're shopping for groceries recall your diet visualization.

Trust and believe in yourself. Maintain a positive attitude. What you think directly affects your body; the mind has a great deal of power. Use that power to your benefit!

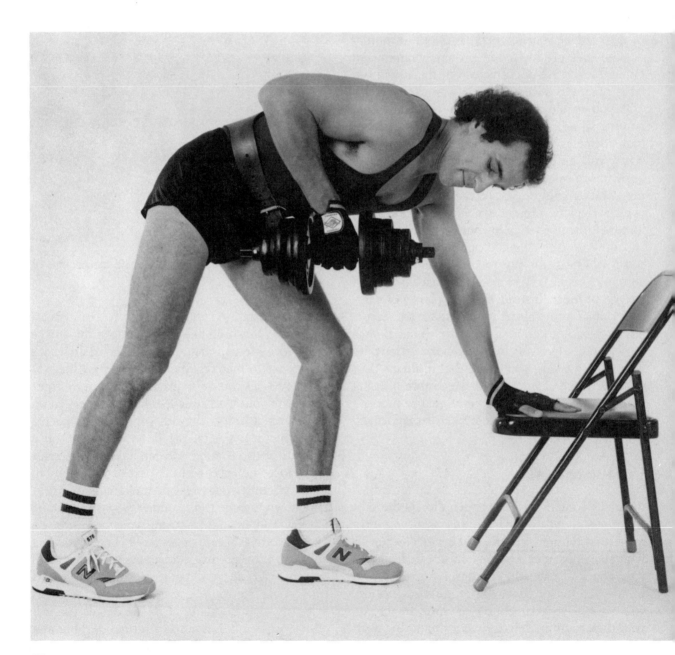

CHAPTER FOUR

Safety

Basic Safety Rules

There are a number of basic safety rules for weight training:

1. For standing exercises, stand with your feet approximately shoulder-width apart, legs straight with knees relaxed. **Don't** lock your knees.

2. Look forward, keeping your chin level.

3. Keep the dumbbells close to your body at all times.

4. Tighten abdominal muscles, squeeze buttocks.

5. Always wear a sturdy pair of athletic shoes while working out.

6. Exhale on the exertion, inhale while bringing the weight back to its starting position. **Don't** hold your breath while lifting.

7. Concentrate on the exercises; avoid distractions.

8. Don't arch your back.

9. Strive for a controlled movement; **don't** jerk the weight.

10. Whenever your joints are supporting your weight or the weight of a dumbbell, don't hyperextend (lock) the joint.

11. Give your muscles a chance to warm up before lifting your maximum weight. You may wish to jog in place, do jumping jacks, ride a stationary bicycle, or do some sit-ups before lifting weights. Specialized warm-ups for each body part are described in chapter 5. Also, as you progress to heavier weights, you should do a light set for the first set with each body part (about a third to a half of your usual weight for that exercise).

12. Don't continue your workout if you feel muscle pain, overly fatigued, or dizzy.

13. Generally, give your body at least twenty-four hours of rest between workouts.

14. Don't try to lift more weight than you can safely handle.

As long as you are careful and follow the above suggestions, you shouldn't have any trouble with injuries. If you do injure a muscle, stop working out immediately and consult the section on treatment of injuries below.

Injury Prevention

If you follow these few simple rules, you can look forward to a lifetime of injury-free strength training. The most important way to prevent injuries is simply to work out correctly. Use good form and don't neglect your warm-up. Read and re-read the above safety rules. In addition, here are some general tips for staying healthy on a weight-training program:

Diet Eat a balanced, nutritious diet. From the point of view of weight training, you should especially make sure you get enough minerals. For more information on diet, as it relates to weight training and general fitness, see chapter 3.

Sleep Get plenty of sleep. It is during sleep that your muscles undergo the beneficial changes brought about by weight training.

Water Drink plenty of fluids (water is ideal) while you're working out, and also when you're not.

Weight belts When doing certain exercises, you may wish to wear a weight belt. Weight belts come in a variety of materials; find one that fits your body and your needs. Weight belts are useful for all chest, back, and shoulder exercises, and leg exercises done in a standing position. Unless you have lower-back trouble, a weight belt is necessary only for those using heavier weights.

Some accessories for a safer workout: water, weight belt, shoes, and weight gloves.

Weightlifting gloves Leather weightlifting gloves, available at sporting-goods stores, provide an element of safety by allowing you to grip the dumbbell better and avoid slippage. In addition, they increase comfort and protect your hands from becoming callused.

Avoid overtraining Overtraining is a common problem that occurs when a person gets too enthusiastic about weight training. It merits a section of its own — read on!

Overtraining

"Overtraining" means working out too often or too much without enough rest and recuperation between sessions. To prevent overtraining:

1. Make sure your workout includes a variety of exercises.

2. Plan your workouts (or use the ones we've designed for you in chapter 8). Avoid rushed or haphazard workouts.

3. Get plenty of sleep. If you're short of sleep, do a lighter workout.

4. Use of alcohol, tobacco, or recreational drugs will reduce the effectiveness of your workouts and increase your susceptibility to overtraining.

5. Every few weeks, give your body a rest by taking a few days off.

6. Be flexible in your attitude toward your workouts. If you really don't have what it takes on a given day, don't force it; try doing a lighter session. But don't let this be an excuse for laziness or repeatedly missing workouts; when possible, meet your commitment to your body!

Signs of Overtraining If you've been working out heavily and experience any of the following symptoms, you may be overtrained and should take a few days off. The following symptoms are listed in order of importance:

1. Elevated resting heart rate. If your resting heart rate (when you wake up in the morning) is consistently higher, by even a few beats, than your normal resting heart rate before you began working out heavily, you probably need to take some time off. (To determine your resting heart rate, count your pulse for 10 seconds and multiply by 6. Do this as soon as you wake up, even before you sit or stand up.)

2. Loss of appetite.

3. Insomnia.

4. Continual soreness in the muscles.

5. Loss of enthusiasm or lethargy, not just toward your workouts but in general.

If you ignore the signs of overtraining, it can lead to injuries and illness. As long as you follow the exercise prescriptions contained in this book, overtraining should not be a problem. Each body is unique, however, and periods of abnormal stress affect your body's responses. Pay attention to the messages your body is sending you and act accordingly.

Recognizing and Managing Injuries

There are four kinds of soreness or pain that can result from lifting weights. The first two below are signs that you're doing it right; the other two mean that you've injured yourself.

"The Burn" Lactic acid builds up in your muscles as you work them. The lactic acid is what prevents you from doing more than 10 or 15 reps. It also causes a slight burning sensation in the muscle, thus the expression "No pain, no gain!" As soon as you finish your set and bring oxygen to the muscle, the lactic acid is dispersed and the sensation disappears.

Localized Soreness It is normal for your muscles to feel sore for 48 to 72 hours after a hard workout. Good ways to relieve soreness are slow stretching, warm compresses, a hot bath, rest, or massage. If the soreness persists for more than three days, you may have strained a muscle.

Strains A strain (or "pulled muscle") usually appears suddenly. It results when the muscle or tendon is over-stretched, resulting in tiny tears. If you follow the safety rules on page 21, pay attention to the principle of balance (pages 13 to 14), and avoid overtraining, strains should not occur.

Should you strain a muscle, first and foremost: **stop your workout**. You'll need at least a few days' rest, more if the strain is severe. When you do pick up your dumbbells again, start out considerably lighter than usual, until you're sure you have completely recovered. The formula for treating strains is RICE — rest, ice, compression, and elevation. Of these, rest and ice are the most important. Aspirin also helps ease pain and reduce swelling. If the strain persists or seems serious, better see your doctor.

Muscle strains heal well with proper attention and rest. But if you don't treat a strain or give yourself time to recover, the injury can become chronic.

Sprains A sprain is a severe injury and is very rare in weight training. It occurs when the ligament is pulled or twisted beyond its maximum range of motion, most often happening in the ankles. A sprain always happens suddenly, and is accompanied by severe bruising and swelling. If you suspect you have a sprain, see your doctor. In the meantime, use the "RICE" treatment mentioned under strains.

Don't be scared off by the above. Weight training is one of the safest forms of exercise if performed correctly — as laid out in this book.

Using push-up bars takes the strain off your wrists and increases range of motion.

CHAPTER FIVE

Warm-Up Exercises

Warming up can protect you from injuries and is an important part of your workout. A warm-up can consist of any activity that significantly raises your heart rate, such as jogging (outside or in place), riding a bicycle (regular or stationary), or jumping rope. In this chapter are some exercises that will generally get your body ready for a training session and specifically warm up the muscles you plan to emphasize in any particular workout. We recommend that you choose one or two warm-up exercises for each body part that you will be exercising on a given day. Each exercise consists of a very simple movement which should be performed several times without stopping. Your warm-up should take about 3 or 4 minutes.

Another aspect of warming up is not covered by these exercises but should be kept in mind as you progress to heavier weights: do a light set for the first set with each body part (about a third to half of your normal weight for that exercise).

Many of the following exercises refer to "aligned position." This means standing with your feet parallel, about shoulder width apart, your shoulders and knees relaxed, your pelvis tucked, and your chin level.

NECK WARM-UPS

Turn

Stand in aligned position. Turn head from side to side as far as you can several times. *(Illus. A)*

Nod

Aligned position. Roll head forward gently, then return to upright position. *(Illus. B)* Don't hunch your shoulders.

A

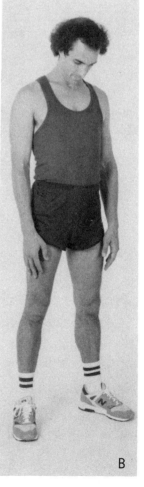

B

SHOULDER AND ARM WARM-UPS

Roll

Aligned position. Roll your shoulders up, back, and down, a few times. Then reverse direction. *(Illus. A)*

A

B

C

Shrug

Aligned position. Lift your shoulders up as high as you can while inhaling, then blow the air out as you abruptly drop your shoulders. *(Not illustrated.)*

Arm Swing

Aligned position. Swing your arms, starting above your head and going down at your sides, and across your chest. *(Illus. B and C)* Then continue the swing up and repeat.

CHEST AND BACK WARM-UPS

Arm Raise to the Front

Aligned position. Link your hands together in front of your body. Inhale deeply as you raise them above your head, exhale as you return to starting position. (*Illus. A*)

Arm Raise to the Rear

Aligned position. Link your hands together in back of your body. Inhale as you raise them up as high as they'll go, exhale as you return to starting position. Don't lean forward at all. (*Illus. B*)

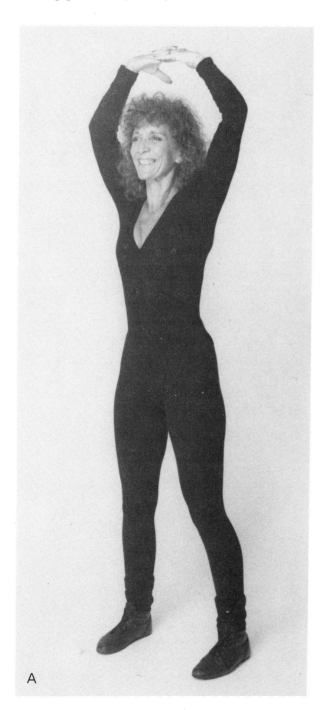

A

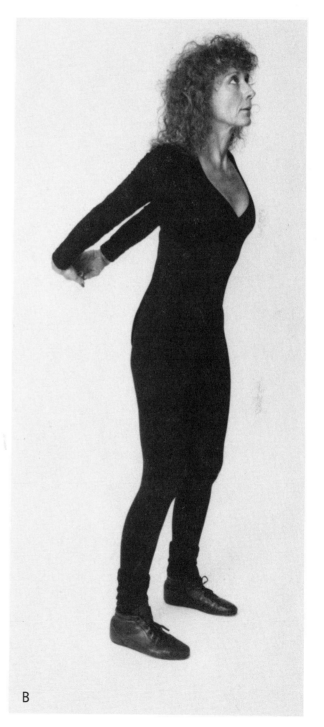

B

Standing Arch-Curl

Aligned position. Start with your arms extended in front of you at chest level, and open them as far as they'll go toward the rear, pulling your shoulder blades together and inhaling. *(Illus. C)* On the exhale, bring your hands back to starting position, rolling your shoulders forward so as to pull your shoulder blades apart. *(Illus. D)*

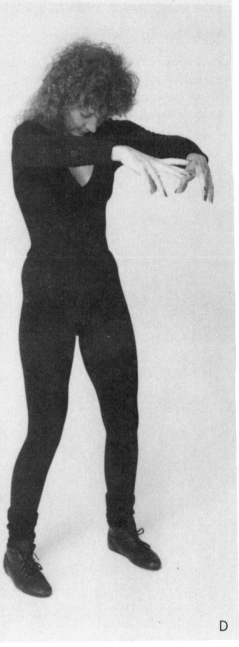

D

C

TORSO WARM-UPS

Twist

Aligned position. Holding your arms straight out to the sides, twist your torso from side to side as fast as you can, keeping your hips stationary and your arms pulled back. *(Illus. A)*

Bent-Arm Twist

Bend your elbows and place each hand on the corresponding shoulder. Twist torso from side to side. *(Illus. B)*

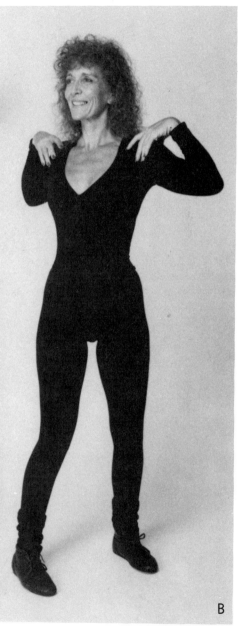

Side Bend

Aligned position. Interlace your hands behind your head and bend from side to side. Keep hips stationary. (*Illus. C*)

Turn-Out

Aligned position, except feet are turned out instead of parallel. Hands on your hips. Keeping your hips stationary, bend from the waist first forward, then back to center (standing), then to the right, back, and to the left in turn. Repeat 3 times then reverse direction. (*Illus. D*)

C

D

Bent-Over Twist

CAUTION: If you have lower-back problems, **avoid** this exercise.

Feet wide, knees somewhat bent, lean forward from the waist, so your torso is parallel to the floor. Interlace your hands behind your head. Bring your left elbow to your right knee, then your right elbow to your left knee. (As with all warm-ups, repeat several times.) Be careful not to arch your back. Allow your hips to be loose so they can move from side to side. *(Illus. E)*

LOWER BACK WARM-UPS

Roll-Down

CAUTION: If you have lower-back problems, **avoid** this exercise.

Aligned position. Drop your head and roll down, vertebra by vertebra, as far as you can, then roll back up. (*See illustration*) Then, keeping your feet stationary, turn your torso toward the left and repeat, then toward the right and repeat. Be careful not to tense your shoulders as you come up.

The Torso Warm-Ups above are also good for warming up the lower-back muscles.

E

LEG WARM-UPS

Standing Leg Extension

Using your right hand for balance, place your left hand on your hip. Extend your left leg to the front, as high as you can. *(Illus. A and B)* Then bend your knee back and forth several times. Repeat with right leg, using left hand to balance. Do *not* lock the knee of the standing leg.

A

B

Dip

Stand on your left leg, place both hands on the floor, and lift your right leg behind you with the knee bent. Dip then lift the left leg by bending the left knee. *(Illus. C and D)* Repeat several times. Keep the left foot flat and don't lock the knee when you lift. Switch legs and repeat.

C

D

HIP WARM-UPS

Swings

Balance with right hand. Swing your left leg forward and back several times, then from side to
side across the front of your body. *(Illus. A and B)*
Switch legs and repeat.

A

B

Side Lunges

Hands on your hips, feet parallel, wide stance. Dip your hips to one side then the other, keeping your feet stationary. Don't lean forward. *(Illus. C)*

C

ANKLE WARM-UP

Ankle Roll

Holding on for balance, lift one leg up and roll the ankle around in one direction several times (*see illustration*), then reverse direction. Switch legs and repeat.

CALF WARM-UP

Lift

Stand on the balls of your feet. Balance yourself with one hand. Lower and lift your heels several times with your feet parallel. *(Illus. A)* Repeat several times with your toes turned out, then with your toes turned in (pigeon-toed). *(Illus. B)*

B

A

Stretching

Stretching is an important part of any exercise program. It helps protect you from injury and keeps your muscles and joints limber. Stretching also relaxes your body and mind; yoga, which is essentially a form of stretching, is regarded in India as a spiritual discipline. Best of all, stretching feels good!

When to Stretch

Ideally, you should insert a stretching session before and after your workout. Stretching before a workout helps relax your muscles and prepare you mentally, while stretching afterwards helps disperse the lactic acid in your muscles, which causes soreness. Remember to warm up your body before you stretch, so as not to put undue stress on your muscles and connective tissue. For some good warm-up suggestions, see chapter 5. If you just have time for one stretching session, we recommend doing it at the end of your workout as a cool-down and to relax your body after the stress of lifting weights. (Contrary to popular belief, it is not essential to stretch before a workout, since the benefits of stretching are long-term and will not prepare you for a particular workout.) Also, if pressed for time you can slip in a few stretches while resting between sets or exercises.

How to Stretch

Stretching should be slow and controlled, with no bouncing or pulsing (short, quick movements). Push yourself, but not to the point where it's painful. Breathe deeply and relax into the stretch. Once you reach your full stretch, hold it for 20 seconds or longer (except as otherwise in-dicated in the descriptions of some stretches). Come out of the stretch slowly, using the same fluid, gradual movement as when you went into the stretch.

NECK STRETCHES

Head Roll

Slowly roll your head forward as far as it will go, put both hands behind your head, and press gently for 3 to 5 seconds. *(Illus. A)*

A

Head Twist

With your chin level, turn your head to the right as far as it will go, hold for a few seconds, then turn as far to the left as you can. Repeat several times. *(Illus. B)*

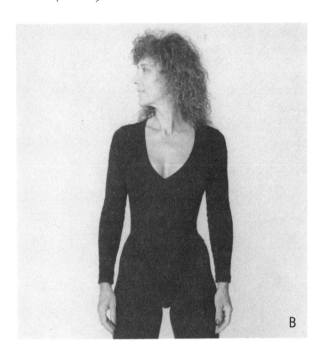

B

Neck Stretch

Extend your right arm straight out from your shoulder, palm facing up. Bring your left ear as close to your left shoulder as you can. Bring your left hand over your head, place it on the right side of your face, and pull gently. Hold for a few seconds, then repeat to the other side. *(Illus. C)*

C

SHOULDER STRETCHES

Shoulder Roll

Slowly roll your shoulders forward, up, back, then down. Repeat a few times, then change direction and repeat a few more times. *(Illus. A)*

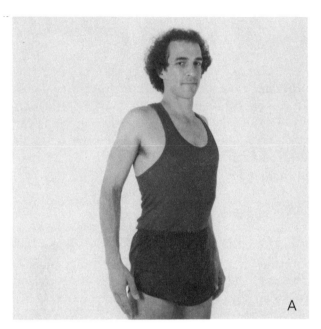

A

Shoulder Circle

Place your hands on top of your shoulders, elbows lifted to the sides. With your elbows, draw circles in the air, a few forward and a few backwards. *(Illus. B)*

B

CHEST STRETCHES

Arch Curl

Stand, knees bent, hands on top of your thighs, shoulders dropped and pulled back, head up. Hold for a few seconds. *(Illus. A)* Slowly round your lower back, roll your shoulders forward, and drop your head. Hold this position for a few seconds. *(Illus. B)* Repeat 2 or 3 times.

B

A

Rib Cage Extension

Standing, extend your arms straight out from your shoulders. Pushing your rib cage to the left, then to the right, reach as far as you can, while keeping your hips stationary. (Do not hold stretch). Repeat a few times. *(Illus. C)*

Doorway Hang

Stand in an open doorway, grasp the door jambs (sides of the door frame) and hang forward as far as you can, allowing your arms to straighten. Hold for 20 seconds. *(Illus. D)*

BACK STRETCHES

Backward Doorway Hang

Stand in an open doorway, grasp the door jambs (sides of the door frame) and hang backwards as far as you can, allowing your arms to straighten. Hold. *(Illus. A)*

Supine Spinal Twist

Lie on your back. Extend your arms to the sides, palms down. Lift your right knee, then bring it across your body and press it towards the floor on your left. Attempt to keep your shoulders flat on the floor and your face turned toward the ceiling. Hold. Repeat on other side. *(Illus. B)*

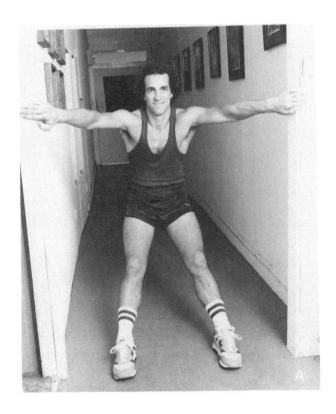

Kneeling Spinal Twist

Kneel on the floor, with your buttocks on your heels, and lean forward. Pull your left arm under your body as far as you can. Turn your head to the right and extend your right arm over the side of your head. Hold and breathe for 20 seconds. Repeat on the other side. *(Illus. C)*

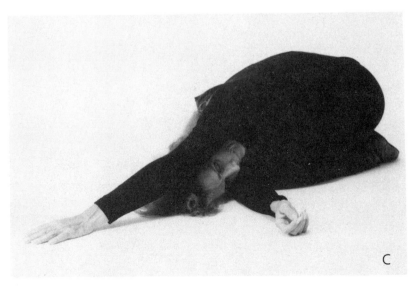

LOWER-BACK STRETCHES

Standing Forward Bend

CAUTION: If you have lower-back problems, **don't** do this stretch.

Stand with your feet about shoulder width apart, making sure that your hips are directly over your ankles. Drop your chin to your chest and continue rolling your spine until you are bent forward as far as you can. Take hold of your legs as close to your ankles as possible, and gently pull your chest towards your thighs. Relax (don't lock) your knees. Allow your head to drop. Hold and breathe for 20 seconds, then roll back up slowly. *(Illus. A)*

Back Curl

Lie on your back. Keeping your right leg extended, pull your left knee towards your chest with your hands. Hold and breathe. *(Illus. B)* Repeat with other leg. (Can also be done with both knees up at once, but make sure the area under your spine is padded.)

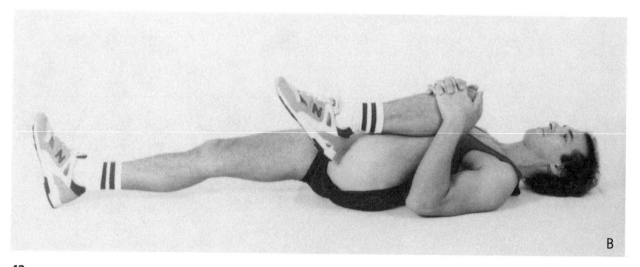

TORSO STRETCHES

Arm Pull

Standing, take hold of your left wrist and pull your arm across the front of your body as far as you can, making sure your left shoulder stays back. Hold. *(Illus. A)* Repeat to other side.

Standing Side Stretch

With your right hand, take hold of your left wrist above your head. Pull to the right as far as you can, allowing your torso to bend but keeping your hips stationary. *(Illus. B)* Repeat to the other side.

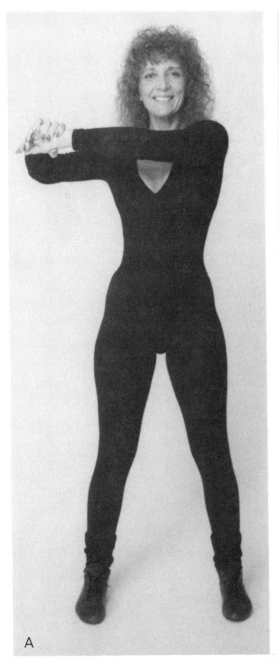

A

B

Seated Side Stretch

Sit with your legs in a wide "V", your back as straight as possible. Flex your right foot, and lean your right forearm on your right thigh. Keeping your left shoulder back, your left hip on the floor, and your chest open, bring your left arm over the top of your head, and stretch over to the right as far as you can. Hold. *(Illus. C)* Repeat to other side.

C

FOREARM STRETCH

Seated Forearm Stretch

Sitting on the floor, place your hands beside your thighs as close to your knees as you can, with your fingers pointing directly backwards. Keep the heels of your hands flat on the floor. *(See illustration)*

LOWER-BODY STRETCHES

Most of the programs in chapter 8 suggest you do one or two stretches "per body part." For those programs, the entire lower body is to be considered one "body part"; choose an exercise from any of the muscle groups below. It is not important which stretch you choose, because any lower-body stretch will have some benefit for all of the muscles in that region.

HIP STRETCHES

Front Hip Stretch

With your left knee and both hands resting on the floor, place your right foot on the floor in front of you so that your right knee is above your right ankle. Push your left hip gently towards the floor until you feel the stretch. *(Illus. A)* Hold and breathe. Repeat with left leg forward.

A

Outer Hip Stretch

Lie face down on the floor, with your right leg extended behind you and your left leg bent so the left calf is underneath your torso. *(Illus. B)* Relax as much as you can, hold the stretch and breathe. (If you don't feel the stretch, move your left foot closer to your arms and head.) Repeat with other leg.

B

One-Legged Hero Pose

Sit on the floor with your left leg extended in front of you. With your right knee bent as much as possible, rest your right leg on your left thigh. Press your chest forward gently, hold and breathe. *(Illus. C)* Reverse legs and repeat.

C

INNER-THIGH STRETCHES

Butterfly

Sitting on the floor with your back straight, knees bent, and the soles of your feet together, slide your heels as close to your body as you can. Place your hands on the floor behind your hips and press your knees toward the floor. Don't bounce. (*Illus. A*)

A

Scissors

Lie on your back. Lift your legs straight up towards the ceiling and open them as far as they'll go into a wide "V". Place your hands on your inner thighs and gently press them a little wider apart. (*Illus. B*)

B

BUTTOCKS STRETCH

Cross-Legged Stretch

Sitting on the floor with your legs crossed, lean your elbows either on top of your calves or on the floor and press forward. (*See illustration*)

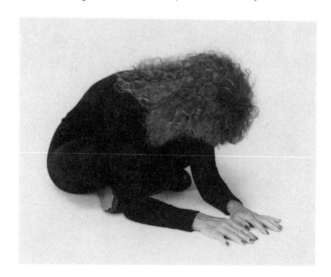

QUADRICEPS (FRONT OF THIGH) STRETCHES

Quad Table Stretch

Stand in front of a table or other similar stable surface about hip height and place your right foot on the edge. Keeping your left foot flat on the floor, press your body forward as far as you can, bending your right knee only as much as you need to. *(Illus. A)* Repeat with other leg. (For those with lower-back problems, **don't** press your body forward. Instead, dip your left leg to achieve the stretch.)

Standing Quad Stretch

Stand on your left leg, balancing with your right hand. Reach back with your left hand, take hold of your right foot, and pull it as close as possible to your buttocks. *(Illus. B)* Keep your knees together. Hold and breathe. Repeat with other leg.

Prone Quad Stretch

Lie face down on the floor. Rest your forehead on your left arm. Reach back with your right hand, take hold of your left foot, and pull it as close to your buttocks as you can, keeping your knees together. Hold and breathe. *(Illus. C)* Repeat with other leg.

C

A

HAMSTRING (BACK OF THIGH) AND KNEE STRETCHES

Good Morning

Stand with feet a little wider than shoulder width apart, knees relaxed. Place your hands on your shoulders. Bending from the waist, and keeping your back flat, bend until your torso is parallel to the floor. Hold for a few seconds. Inhale as you bend down, exhale as you come up. Repeat a few times. *(Illus. A)* NOTE: If you have lower-back problems, use caution.

Hamstring Stretch

Rest your left foot and lower portion of calf on a surface high enough so your leg is parallel to the floor. Holding on to your calf, slowly press your chest towards your left leg until you feel the stretch. Hold and breathe. *(Illus. B)* Repeat with right leg. NOTE: For those with lower-back problems, don't press your chest forward. Instead, dip your standing leg to achieve the stretch.

B

Seated Forward Bend

CAUTION: Don't do this stretch if you have lower-back problems.

Sit on the floor, back straight, legs extended in front of you, feet slightly flexed, hands on top of your knees to prevent them from bending. Exhaling, press your chest as close to your thighs as you can. Hold and breathe. *(Illus. C)*

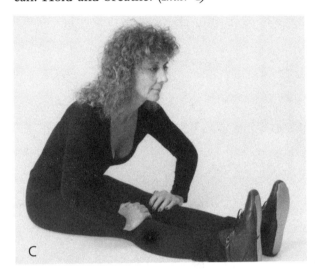

CALF STRETCHES

Wall Stretch

Facing a wall or sturdy object, lean against it with your hands. Place your feet as far away as you can, keeping your heels flat on the floor. *(Illus. A)*

Floor Stretch

With both hands and feet on the floor, walk your hands forward as far as you can, keeping your heels flat on the floor. Don't lock your elbows. *(Illus. B)*

ANKLE STRETCHES

Ankle Roll

Sit in a chair, right foot on the floor. Support your left calf in front of your torso with your left hand. With your right hand, hold on to your left foot, and rotate it in circles, several times in one direction and then several in the other direction. *(Illus. A)* Make sure that your hand does the work; let your ankle relax. Reverse position and repeat.

Flex Point

Stand on your right foot, bracing yourself against a wall or any stable object for balance. Lift your left foot off the floor slightly, flex it, and hold for a few seconds. *(Illus. B)* Then point the foot and hold. Repeat 2 or 3 times. Reverse feet.

Achilles Dip

Stand with the ball of your right foot on the edge of a step. *(Illus. C)* Bracing with your hands for balance, press the right heel as far toward the floor as you can. Repeat with the other foot.

CHAPTER SEVEN

Weight Exercises

The descriptions of each exercise in this chapter take you through one complete "set" of the exercise. Most of the programs in chapter 8 call for you to do 2 to 4 sets of each exercise. After completing the exercise instructions, rest, then repeat the exercise as indicated in your program. As a general guideline, the best all-around workout strategy is to do 3 or 4 sets of an exercise, with 8 to 12 repetitions per set.

Exercises for Legs and Buttocks

STANDING EXERCISES

The following standing leg exercises suggest use of a dumbbell or pair of dumbbells. For beginners, all these exercises can be done without weights. As soon as you are able, try them with dumbbells.

Standard Squat

(works entire legs and buttocks)

Starting Position Stand with your feet a little wider than shoulder width apart, parallel to each other. Hold the dumbbells at your hips. *(Illus. A)* If you have a barbell you may use it on this exercise. Take the barbell from the rack and hold it across your shoulders, being careful not to let it rest on your neck vertebrae.

Movement

1. Inhale and lower your body as low as you can comfortably go, or until your thighs are parallel to the floor. Do **not** go lower than this or you will put too much stress on your knees. *(Illus. B)*
2. Exhale as you squeeze your buttocks and come back to the standing position.
3. Repeat for prescribed number of repetitions.

A

B

Notes
- Keep your spine straight during the entire movement.
- Don't lean forward more than necessary to keep your balance.
- Keep your feet flat on the floor. If you are unable to do this, elevate your heels using a book about an inch thick.
- If it feels more comfortable to you, particularly as you progress to heavier weights, hold the dumbbells at your sides with arms relaxed.

Variation Front Squat: Place your feet together and keep your knees together *(Illus. C and D)*; otherwise follow all directions as above.

C

D

Wide Turn-Out Squat
(works inner thighs and buttocks)

Starting Position Stand with your feet about twice shoulder width apart, toes pointing outward. Hold the dumbbells together at your hips *(Illus. A)* or in front of you with arms extended downwards and elbows relaxed.

Movement

1. Inhale as you lower your body until your thighs are parallel to the floor. *(Illus. B)* Do **not** go lower than this or you will put too much stress on your knees.

2. Squeeze your buttocks and come back to the standing position (exhale).

3. Repeat for prescribed number of repetitions.

Notes
• Keep your spine straight during the entire movement.
• Do not bend your arms or lift the dumbbells with your arms.
• Never allow the knees to go forward of the ankles.

A

B

Pole Squat

(works entire legs and buttocks)

Starting Position Find an upright beam, pole, banister, or door handle around or through which you can loop a kitchen towel. Place your feet a little wider than shoulder width apart. With one hand, hold both ends of the looped towel. With the other hand, hold a single dumbbell in front of your chest. *(Illus. A)*

Movement

1. Lower your body (inhaling) until your thighs are parallel to the floor. *(Illus. B)* Do **not** go lower than this or you will put too much stress on your knees.

2. Squeeze your buttocks and come back to standing position (exhale).

3. Repeat for prescribed number of repetitions.

Notes

• Pull on the towel to brace yourself.
• Keep your spine erect during the entire movement.
• Keep your feet flat on the floor.
• Don't lean back.

A

B

Standard Lunge
(works entire leg, buttocks, and outer hip)

Starting Position Hold dumbbells on your hips. Stand facing a stair or elevated area. *(Illus. A)* If you have a barbell, you can use it on this exercise as with Standard Squat (see page 52).

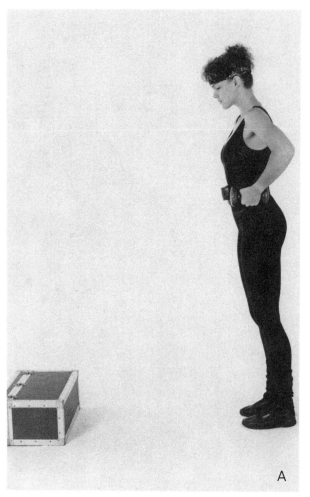

A

B

Movement
1. Lunge forward, making sure the entire foot steps onto the elevated area (inhale).
2. Press the back knee toward the floor. *(Illus. B)*
3. Step back to starting position (exhale).
4. Repeat with other leg and continue alternating legs until you have performed the desired number of repetitions with each leg.

Notes
• Position yourself so that the lunging knee is directly over the ankle at the lowest point of the movement.
• Keep back straight throughout the entire movement.
• If no elevated area or step is available, this exercise can be performed on a level floor. CAUTION: People with knee problems are advised to perform lunges **only** onto an elevated area.

Variation Instead of going back to starting position, keep the same leg forward and dip up and down, for the desired number of repetitions, by straightening and bending the forward leg. Then repeat with the other leg forward.

Side Lunge

(works hips, outer and inner thighs, and buttocks)

Starting Position Feet close together and parallel, hold dumbbells at hips. *(Illus. A)*

2. Press left knee forward slightly to further work the hip and buttocks muscles. *(Illus. B)*
3. Return to starting position (exhale).
4. Repeat with right leg. Continue alternating legs for desired number of repetitions.

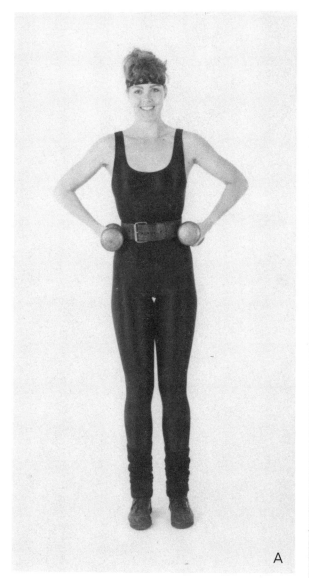

A

B

Movement

1. Lunge sideways to your left as far as you can, keeping both feet flat on the floor and parallel (inhale).

Notes

• Do not roll the stationary foot; keep both feet flat on the floor at all times.
• Be careful not to lean forward from the hips.

Step-Up
(works hips, thighs, and buttocks)

Starting Position Find a stool, low chair, sturdy box, or other object that can support your weight. Brace it against a wall if necessary. An elevated area about 18 inches high can serve also. Hold the dumbbells against your hips. Face the stool or elevated area.

Movement

1. Step up onto the stool with your right foot. *(Illus. A)*

2. Step up with your left foot so that you are standing on the stool (exhale). *(Illus. B)*

3. Step down (backwards) with your right foot.

4. Step down with your left foot.

5. Repeat, beginning with left leg, and continue alternating legs. Always begin your step down on the same foot with which you began the step up.

Notes

• Do not let your arms hang down or swing. This can cause you to lose your balance.

• Place your entire foot on the surface you are stepping onto (not just the ball of your foot).

• Perform this exercise slowly and carefully to make sure you do not lose your balance and fall.

Stair Climbing
(works thighs, calves, and buttocks)

This exercise can only be done if you live in a two-storey house or have access to a flight of stairs.

Starting Position Hold the dumbbells against your hips. Stand at the bottom of a flight of stairs.

Movement

1. Run up the stairs.

2. Come down slowly.

3. Catch your breath and then repeat. Each trip up and down the stairs counts as one "set" of this exercise.

Notes

• Don't swing your arms or you may lose your balance.

• Do not do this exercise on the balls of your feet. Your feet must step firmly and flatly on each step.

A

B

FLOOR EXERCISES

Joy Kick
(works hips, buttocks, and outer thigh)

Starting Position Balance on left hand and knee, with your right leg extended parallel to the floor. Place your right hand on your hip. Keep your chest open. *(Illus. A)* This exercise does not use dumbbells—it's hard enough as it is!

Movement
1. With toes pointed, bend your right leg at the knee. *(Illus. B)*
2. Straighten the leg, keeping toes pointed.
3. Repeat for the desired number of repetitions.

4. Repeat entire exercise with right foot flexed instead of pointed.
5. Change legs and repeat steps 1 through 4.
6. Start with 20 repetitions pointing and 20 flexed, count down 5 at a time (second set 15 reps, third set 10, last set 5 reps). Beginners should start with less than 20 reps, follow same pattern.

Notes
• Don't feel bad if you can't start out at 20 reps—do the best you can.
• When bending your leg, bring your heel as close to your buttocks as possible.
• Move slowly—don't rely on momentum!
• The supporting elbow should not be locked.

A

B

Fire Hydrant with Dumbbell

(works hips and buttocks)

Starting Position Begin on your hands and knees. Place a dumbbell behind the right knee and hold it in place by bending the leg. *(Illus. A)* Beginners need not use dumbbell.

Movement

1. Lift your right leg straight out to the side from the hip (exhale). *(Illus. B)*

2. Return to starting position (inhale).

3. Repeat for desired number of repetitions.

4. Repeat with left leg.

Notes

• Hold your abdominal muscles tight to support the back.

• Hold the dumbbell firmly with your leg.

• For those with weak wrists, this exercise can be performed leaning on your forearm.

Knee Lift to the Rear with Dumbbell
(works back of thigh and buttocks)

Starting Position Begin on your hands and knees. Place a dumbbell behind the right knee and hold it in place by bending the leg. *(Illus. A)* Beginners need not use dumbbell.

Movement
1. Lift your right leg directly behind you until the right thigh is parallel to the floor (exhale). *(Illus. B)*
2. Return to starting position (inhale).
3. Perform desired number of repetitions.
4. Repeat with left leg.

Notes
• Hold your abdominal muscles tight to support the back.
• Hold the dumbbell firmly with your leg.
• For those with weak wrists, this exercise can be performed leaning on your forearm.
• Do **not** lift your thigh higher than parallel to the floor, as it can be stressful for the lower back.

A

B

Inner Thigh Series
(works inner thigh)

Because this exercise has multiple variations built into the basic exercise description, you need only do one set.

Starting Position Lie on your right side, upper arm on floor, head resting in your hand. (If this position causes neck strain, lie flat with your arm outstretched, head resting on your arm.) Bring right leg forward as far as you can, with your foot flexed. Keep your left leg straight. With your left hand, hold a dumbbell against your inner right thigh. Beginners need not use dumbbell.

Movement
1. Lift your right leg as high as you can, then lower it, for the correct number of repetitions. *(Illus. A)*
2. Repeat with right foot pointed.

3. Bend your left leg, left knee pointed toward ceiling, left foot flat on the floor in back of your right leg. Extend your right leg straight down from the torso, foot flexed, dumbbell resting on inner right thigh.
4. Lift your right leg as high as you can, then lower it, for the given number of repetitions. *(Illus. B)*
5. Repeat step 4 with right foot pointed.
6. Bring your left leg in front of your right leg and repeat steps 4 and 5. *(Illus. C)*
7. Repeat entire exercise lying on your left side, legs reversed.

Notes
- Top hip stays rotated forward throughout exercise.
- Do not support the dumbbell in your hand; just use your hand to hold the weight in place.

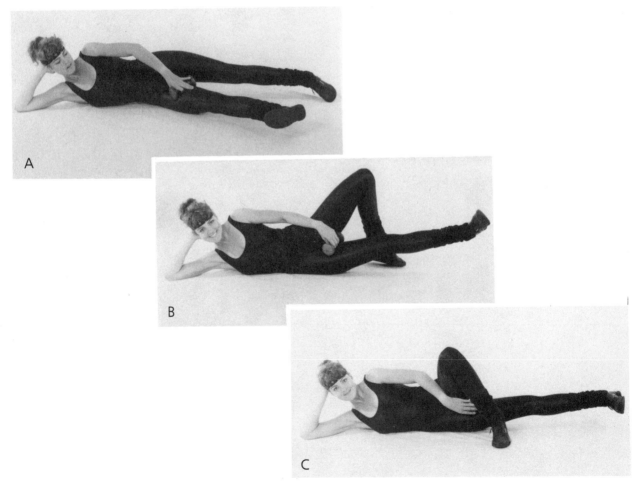

⅔ Side Leg Lift
(works outer thigh)

Starting Position   Lie on your left side, left upper arm on floor, head in hand. (If this position causes neck strain, lie flat with your arm outstretched, head resting on your arm.) Bring both legs forward ⅔ of the way. Bend left (bottom) knee, extend right (top) leg. Flex right foot. Hold the dumbbell on the outer right thigh, as close to the knee as possible. *(Illus. A)* Beginners need not use dumbbell.

Movement
1. Lift your right leg ⅔ of the way up, hold briefly. *(Illus. B)*
2. Lower leg slowly to the floor. Perform prescribed number of repetitions.

3. Repeat with right foot pointed.
4. Again lift right leg ⅔ of the way up, then point foot, flex again, and lower leg. Do this for the given number of reps.
5. Put down the dumbbell. The last step of the exercise is performed without weight.
6. Rotate front of right thigh toward floor. Bend right knee slightly. With foot flexed, kick the right foot a few inches in a pulsing motion for the desired number of reps. *(Illus. C)*
7. Lie on your right side and repeat entire series.

Notes
• Keep the top hip rotated forward throughout the entire exercise.
• Do not lift the leg more than ⅔ of the way. Otherwise the joint is doing the work, instead of the intended muscle.

A

B

C

Quad Lift
(works front of thigh)

Because this exercise has multiple variations built into the basic exercise description, you need only do one set.

Starting Position   Sit up as straight as you can, left knee bent, right leg extended in front of you on the floor. Place left hand behind you, leaning on it as little as possible. With right hand, hold the dumbbell on the right thigh as close to the knee as you can reach. Flex the right foot. Beginners need not use dumbbell.

Movement
1. Lift right leg as high as you can and lower slowly, for given number of repetitions. *(See illustration)*
2. Repeat with foot pointed.
3. Switch dumbbell to left leg and repeat steps 1 and 2 with left leg.
4. Repeat steps 1 through 3, performing five less repetitions each.

Notes
• Don't lock the elbow you're leaning on or tense the supporting shoulder.
• Contract your abdominals (stomach muscles) to support your lower back.

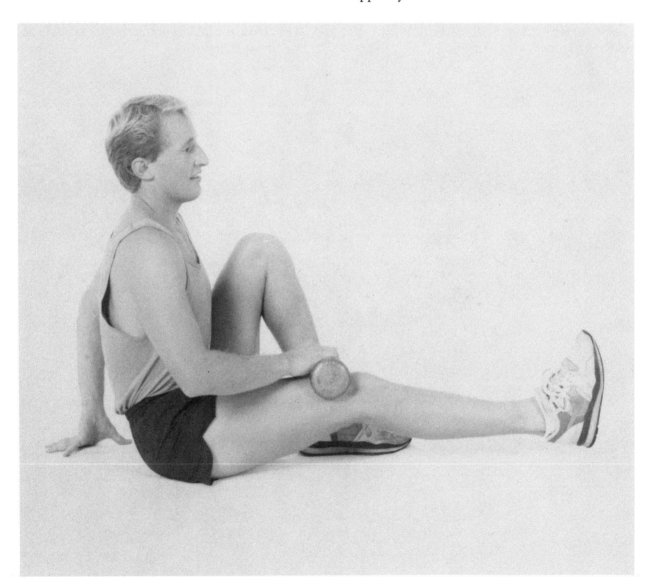

Seated Leg Extension, on Home Gym Equipment
(works front of thigh)

Starting Position Follow directions that come with equipment. Sit with feet under padded rollers.

Movement
1. Exhale as you lift your legs out to a fully extended position, as shown in photograph.
2. Lower slowly as you inhale.
3. Repeat for given number of repetitions.

Notes
• Don't lock your knees when legs are extended.
• Keep abdominals tight throughout the exercise.

Padded rollers on gym equipment protect the lower legs when doing Seated Leg Extensions.

Pelvic Tilt
(works buttocks and entire leg, especially inner thigh)

Starting Position Lie on your back, legs bent at the knees, feet flat on the floor about shoulder width apart. With one hand hold the dumbbell against the pubic bone.

Movement
1. Lift your tailbone off the floor. *(See illustration)*

2. With the tailbone lifted, "pulse" your pelvis up and down in quick, short movements for the given number of repetitions, keeping buttocks tight.
3. Lower your tailbone to the floor and quickly bring your legs together so that only your toes and knees are touching.
4. Lift your tailbone and repeat step 2 for the given number of reps.
5. Lower your tailbone and bring your heels together so that your heels, toes, and knees are all touching.
6. Lift your tailbone and repeat step 2 for the given number of reps.
7. Lower your tailbone again to the floor, and turn your toes outward so that your heels only are touching.
8. Lift your tailbone again and repeat step 2 for the given number of reps.

CAUTION: **Do not** lift your lower back off the floor while doing this exercise; just lift the tailbone as shown in the illustration.

Double Leg Curl
(works back of thigh)

Starting Position   Lie face down on the floor. Cross your hands on the floor and place your forehead on top of your hands. Bend your knees and hold the dumbbell between your feet. *(See illustration)*

Movement
1. Slowly lower your feet to the floor (inhale).
2. Slowly bring your feet back up to starting position (exhale).
3. Repeat for given number of repetitions. This constitutes one "set."

4. Rest for a minute.
5. Perform a total of 3 or 4 sets.

Notes
• Keep buttocks contracted to protect the lower back.
• Make sure the dumbbell is held firmly with your feet so that it does not fall onto your back.
• You will find you can do this exercise with a heavier dumbbell than the other floor exercises, but first make sure you have mastered it so there is no danger of dropping the dumbbell.

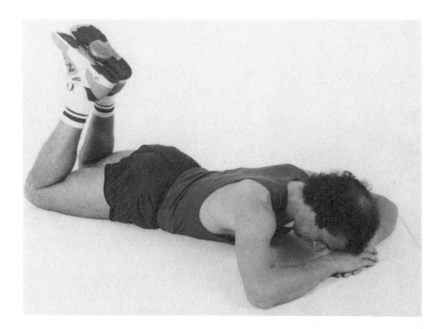

Hamstring Flexor, on Home Gym Equipment
(works back of thigh)

Starting Position   Follow directions that come with the equipment. Lie face down with ankles under padded rollers.

Movement
1. Exhale as you curl your feet toward your buttocks, as shown in the photograph.
2. Inhale as you lower the legs slowly.
3. Repeat for given number of reps.

Note   Try to keep hips flat on bench.

Hamstring Flexors can be done in place of Leg Curls, if you have the equipment.

Back Exercises

Good Morning
(works lower back and abdominals)

CAUTION: This exercise, while valuable for strengthening the lower back, can put stress on that area, which is a weak link in many people. Start with very light dumbbells, or none at all, and work your way up gradually. If you've had low-back problems in the past, consult your orthopedist before doing this one. Regardless of your history, don't push yourself on this exercise. It helps to do this exercise (or one of the other lower-back exercises—Dead Lift and Straight-Leg Dead Lift) regularly. If you feel any discomfort, stop immediately.

Starting Position　Stand, knees straight but not locked, feet about shoulder width apart, pelvis tucked. Rest dumbbells on top of your shoulders, holding them in place with your hands throughout the exercise. Keep your chin up. *(Illus. A)*

Movement

1. Inhale as you bend over from the waist until your torso is parallel to the floor. Keep your back as straight as possible and make sure your hips and ankles stay aligned. *(Illus. B)*

2. Exhale as you slowly return to starting position. Do not lean over backwards.

3. Repeat for prescribed number of reps.

Note　Remember not to lock or bend your knees.

A

B

Dead Lift
(works lower back, buttocks, and thighs)

CAUTION: This exercise is very valuable for strengthening the lower back, but it can cause injury to that region if performed with too much weight. Start with very light dumbbells (or none at all) and work your way up gradually. If you've had low-back problems in the past, consult your orthopedist before doing this one. Regardless of your history, don't push yourself on this exercise. Do it near the start of your workout, before you tire yourself out with other exercises, and give it your full concentration. It also helps to do this exercise or one of the other lower-back exercises (Good Morning and Straight-Leg Dead Lift) regularly. If you feel any discomfort, stop immediately.

Starting Position   This exercise can be done with dumbbells, or with a barbell if you have one. Standing with your feet about shoulder width apart, bend over and drop your buttocks so your thighs are roughly parallel to the floor. Hold the dumbbells (or bar) just above your feet, arms on the outside of your calves, chin up. *(Illus. A)*

Movement
1. Exhale as you slowly pull the dumbbells (or bar) up along the front of your legs and straighten your body. *(Illus. B and C)*
2. Inhaling, **slowly** reverse the movement as precisely as you can, keeping your knees open. Keep your head up.
3. Repeat for prescribed number of reps.

A

B

Notes

- Keep arms straight throughout the exercise (but do not lock elbows).
- Don't lean back when you come up to standing position.
- Keep the dumbbells close to your body at all times.

C

Straight-Leg Dead Lift
(works lower back and thighs)

See CAUTION note contained in the description of regular Dead Lift exercise, above)

Starting Position This exercise can be done with dumbbells, or with a barbell if you have one. Stand with feet shoulder width apart. Bend over at the waist, keeping your legs as straight as you can without locking the knees. Hold the dumbbells beside your feet on the floor or as close to the floor as you can. If you're using a barbell, bend over at the waist and grasp the bar from the top, hands at hip width. Hold your head up. *(Illus. A)*

A

Movement

1. Bring your body up to an erect posture, while keeping your back as straight as you can (exhale). *(Illus. B and C)*

2. Reverse movement and return to starting position (inhale). Keep your head up.

3. Repeat for prescribed number of reps.

Notes

• Keep arms straight throughout exercise (but do not lock elbows).

• Don't bend your legs as you lift or lower the weights.

C

B

70

Bent-Over Row

(works latissimus dorsi, "lats" — the major back muscles)

Starting Position   Lean on the edge of a chair with your left hand. Hold a dumbbell in your right hand, arm extended straight down toward the floor. Keep your shoulders parallel to the floor. *(Illus. A)*

Movement
1. Pull the dumbbell straight up until it is beside your chest, keeping the arm close to your body at all times (exhale). *(Illus. B)*
2. Slowly lower the weight to starting position (inhale).

3. Repeat for prescribed number of reps.
4. Switch arms and repeat steps 1 through 3.

Notes
• Don't arch your back.
• Keep your abdominals contracted.

Variations
A. Bent-Over Rows can be done with both arms at once, or with a barbell. This works your upper back more. Be extra careful not to arch your back.
B. To work the lower latissimus as well, forget about keeping your shoulders parallel to the floor, and let the weight down in step 2 until it's just an inch or two from the floor. (This variation cannot be used when doing the exercise with a barbell.)

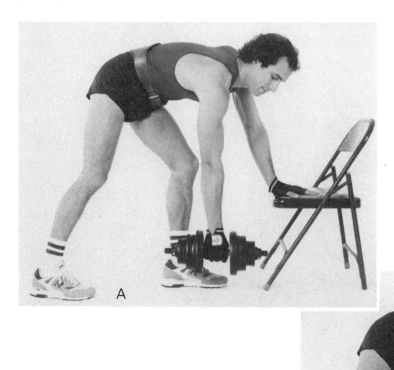

One-Arm Reverse Fly
(works upper back and rear shoulder muscle)

Starting Position   Lean on the edge of a chair with your left hand. Hold a dumbbell in your right hand, arm extended straight down towards the floor. Keep your shoulders parallel to the floor. *(Illus. A)*

Movement
1. With your right elbow bent slightly, raise the dumbbell out to your side, in a semicircle, bringing it a little higher than your back (exhale). *(Illus. B)*

2. Slowly lower the dumbbell, by the same path, to starting position (inhale).

3. Repeat for prescribed number of reps.

4. Reverse arms, repeat steps 1 through 3.

Notes
- Hold your torso still.
- As you lower the dumbbell, be careful not to swing it. Lower the weight slower than you lifted it.

Upright Row

(works inner and upper back)

Starting Position Stand, knees straight but not locked, feet shoulder width apart, pelvis tucked. Hold dumbbells (or barbell, if you have one) in front of your thighs, palms facing towards you. *(Illus. A)*

Movement

1. Pull the weights up along the front of your body until they are in front of your shoulders, lifting your elbows as high as you can (exhale). *(Illus. B)*

2. Slowly return to starting position (inhale).

3. Repeat for prescribed number of reps.

Notes

• The handles of the dumbbells should be parallel to the floor.

• Keep your chin level.

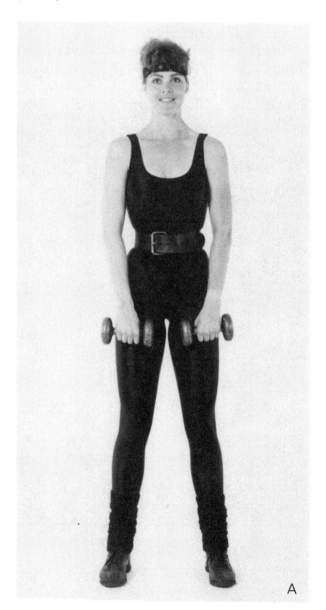

Shrug

(works the trapezius—muscle between your shoulders)

Starting Position   Stand, knees straight but not locked, feet shoulder width apart, pelvis tucked. Hold dumbbells in front of your thighs or at your sides, palms facing in. *(Illus. A)*

Movement

1. Roll your shoulders forward and up as high as you can (exhale). *(Illus. B)*
2. Roll the shoulders to the rear and down to starting position (inhale).
3. Repeat for prescribed number of reps.

Note   Unlike most exercises, the negative motion (step 2) can be more rapid than the exertion (step 1).

Lat Pull-Down, on Cable Equipment

(works upper and outer back)

Starting Position   Follow directions that come with the equipment. Sit on stool, grasp ends of bar.

Movement

1. Exhale as you pull the bar down behind your neck, as shown in the photograph.
2. Inhale as you slowly return the bar to the starting position.
3. Repeat for given number of repetitions.

Notes

• Don't arch your back.
• Use different grips and widths as you like. (Follow suggestions that come with the equipment.)

With cable equipment, you can include the Lat Pull-Down in your workout.

Exercises for Chest

Push-Up from the Knees

There are several ways to do push-ups. This one is the easiest. Most women will find that this version is sufficient to effectively exercise the chest muscles (pectorals).

NOTE: Inexpensive "push-up bars" are available in sporting goods stores for about $10. We recommend these to take the pressure off your wrists and increase the range of motion and effectiveness of push-ups. They can be used for standard or from-the-knees push-ups. The use of push-up bars is illustrated on page 23.

Starting Position   Lie face down on the floor. Be sure your knees are padded (use a towel, carpet, mat, or type of cushion). Position your hands beside your chest. Lift your calves off the floor a few inches and cross your ankles. Look forward. *(Illus. A)*

Movement

1. Keeping your knees on the floor, exhale as you push your body up until your arms are extended. *(Illus. B)*

2. Inhale as you slowly lower yourself to starting position.

3. Repeat as many times as you can without stopping. (This constitutes one set.)

Notes

• Keep your torso straight (it helps to contract the abdominals).
• Don't lock your elbows.
• Keep your elbows near your sides.

Variation   To emphasize inner chest and triceps, push-ups can also be done with the hands close together (about 4 inches apart).

A

B

Standard Push-Up

Starting Position Lie face down on the floor. Position your hands beside your chest. Flex your feet so that the balls of your feet are touching the floor. Look forward. *(Illus. A)* Again, inexpensive "push-up bars" are recommended to take the pressure off your wrists and increase the range of motion and effectiveness of push-ups.

Movement
1. Push your body up until your arms are extended (exhale). *(Illus. B)*
2. Slowly lower yourself to starting position (inhale).
3. Repeat as many times as you can without stopping. (This constitutes one set.)

Notes
• Keep your torso straight (it helps to contract the abdominals).
• Don't lock your elbows.
• Keep your elbows near your sides.

Variations
A. To emphasize inner chest and triceps, push-ups can also be done with the hands close together (about 4 inches apart).
B. Once you are able to do 15 push-ups per set, you can make the exercise tougher by placing your feet on a stool or chair. This version also puts more emphasis on the shoulder muscles. Another technique to increase the resistance is to put a heavy dictionary on your upper back.

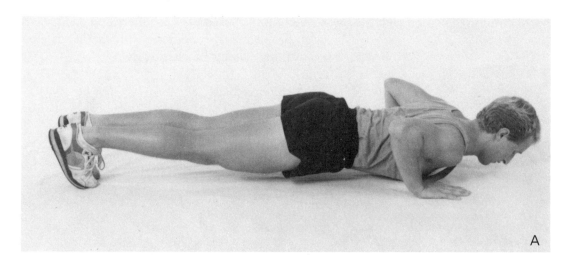

A

B

Dumbbell Press

This exercise and the two that follow are home versions of exercises usually done on a padded weight bench. If you have one, or if you can rig up a picnic bench with towels or a blanket as padding, you will probably find it worthwhile to use it instead of lying on the floor with your back propped up with pillows. When doing this exercise on a bench, start with the elbows fully bent so that the dumbbells are at shoulder level.

Starting Position   Lie on the floor, knees bent up, two pillows or cushions positioned under your upper back. Hold a dumbbell in each hand, palms facing forward as if you were holding a bar, elbows extended out to the sides. Hold the dumbbells directly over your shoulders, upper arms resting on the floor. *(Illus. A)*

Movement
1. Press the dumbbells up and toward each other as you exhale, touching them together at arm's length above your chest. *(Illus. B)*
2. Inhale as you return to starting position.
3. Repeat for prescribed number of reps.

Notes
• Keep the dumbbells directly over your chest, **not** over your face or stomach.
• Don't bend your wrists.
• Squeeze your chest muscles at the top of the movement.
• Concentrate! If you feel yourself getting weak before the last rep, **stop** so as not to risk dropping the dumbbells.

Variation   Turn your wrists so that your palms are facing each other, and perform the exercise as above.

A

B

77

Bench Press with Barbell

(for those with barbell and bench set)

Starting Position Lie on the bench, feet flat on the floor, bar over the bridge of your nose, hands 2½ to 3 feet apart. Lift bar up and out from the rack.

Movement

1. Inhale as you slowly lower the bar to your chest (just above the nipple line) as shown in the photograph.

2. Exhale as you push the bar straight up.

Notes

- Don't arch your back.
- You might prefer to place your feet on the bench instead of the floor, to facilitate a flat back.
- Don't lock your elbows at the up portion of the press.
- Grip can be narrowed to work triceps more, or widened to work outer chest. Angle of bench may be adjustable to emphasize upper chest. Follow suggestions that come with equipment.

If you have the equipment, a Bench Press is a good substitute for Push-Ups.

Fly

Starting Position   Lie on the floor, knees bent up, two pillows or cushions positioned under your upper back. Hold a dumbbell in each hand, directly above your chest, dumbbells touching, palms facing each other, elbows somewhat bent. *(Illus. A)* NOTE: Use a bench or other substitute if available — see Dumbbell Press above.

Movement

1. Keeping your elbows somewhat bent, open your arms until your elbows touch the floor (inhale). The dumbbells should trace a semicircle as they descend. *(Illus. B)* If using a bench, allow the weights to descend until they are at the same level as your torso.

2. Bring the dumbbells back to starting position by the same semicircular path, as if you were hugging a big tree.

3. Repeat for prescribed number of reps.

Variation   Turn your wrists so that your palms are facing forward, and perform the exercise as above. This makes the exercise slightly harder and you will probably have to use lighter dumbbells than for regular flyes.

A

B

Pullover

Starting Position   Lie on the floor, knees bent up, two pillows or cushions positioned under your upper back. Hold a single dumbbell at arm's length above your chest, with both hands, palms up, wrapped around the end of the dumbbell. *(Illus. A)* Use a bench if available — see Dumbbell Press above.

Movement
1. Allowing the elbows to bend only a little, slowly lower the dumbbell toward the floor until it touches the floor (inhale). *(Illus. B)* (Don't let it rest on the floor.) If using a bench, lower the weight as far as you safely can.
2. Keeping the arms almost straight, slowly raise the dumbbell back up to starting position (exhale).
3. Repeat for prescribed number of reps.

Note   If you need more weight than your heaviest single dumbbell, use two at a time. Hold both dumbbells with both hands at once. CAUTION: Don't try this unless you're sure you can get a good grip and won't drop the weights.

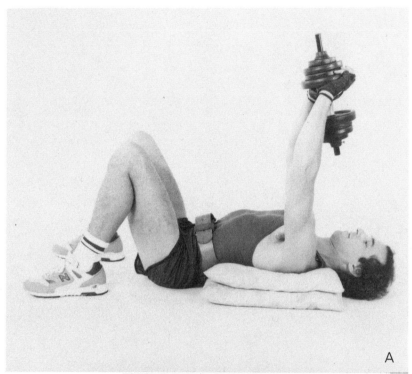

A

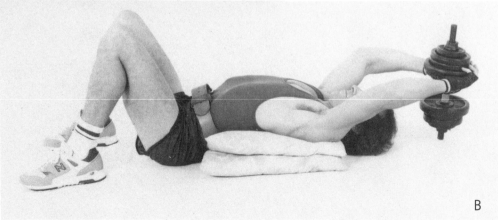

B

Exercises for Shoulders

When working the shoulders, be especially careful not to arch your back.

Shoulder Press
(works top of shoulder)

Starting Position   Sit in a chair. Hold dumbbells at shoulder height, close to your body, palms facing forward. *(Illus. A)* If you prefer to use a barbell, you may hold it in front of the neck or behind the neck; alternate between workouts for variety.

Movement
1. Exhale as you press both dumbbells (or bar) straight up to arm's length. *(Illus. B)*
2. Inhale as you slowly lower weights to starting position.
3. Repeat for desired number of reps.

Note   Keep your feet planted firmly on the floor.

Variations
A. This exercise can be done standing if you prefer. However, as you progress to heavier weights you will find it easier to keep your balance while seated.
B. You might also try the exercise with palms facing in instead of forward, for variety.
C. Can be done alternating arms instead of both at once. (If you choose to alternate arms, remember to do twice as many movements per set — you must do the prescribed number of reps with *each* arm.) Don't lean from side to side.
D. You can also do an entire set with one arm, then a set with the other arm, and so on. Don't lean from side to side.

A

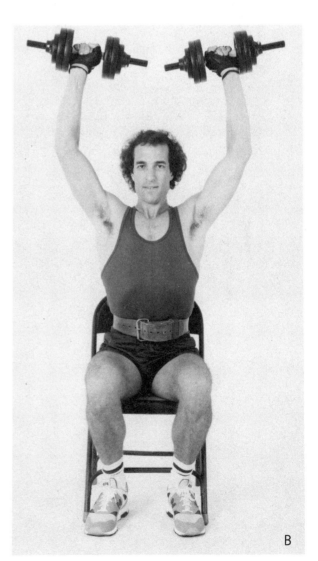

B

Arnold Press
(works top and front of shoulder)

As you may have guessed, this press is named after Arnold Schwarzenegger, a seven-time Mr. Olympia turned actor.

Starting Position   Sit in a chair. Hold dumbbells in front of you at shoulder height, close to your body, palms facing toward you. (Illus. A)

Movement
1. Press both dumbbells up to arm's length, gradually turning them as you go so that at the top of the movement your palms are facing away from you (exhale). (Illus. B)

2. Lower dumbbells to starting position, gradually turning your wrists so that your palms are facing back towards you again.

3. Repeat for desired number of reps.

Note   Keep your feet planted firmly on the floor.

Variation   This exercise can be done standing if you prefer. However, as you progress to heavier weights you will find it easier to keep your balance while seated.

A

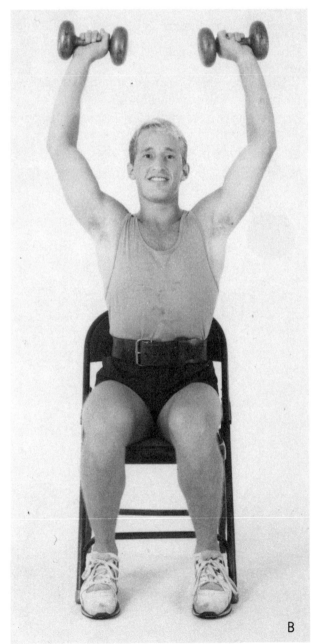

B

Side Lateral
(works outer shoulder)

Starting Position Sit holding dumbbells at your sides, palms facing in towards you, arms relaxed. *(Illus. A)*

Movement
1. With arms straight but elbows relaxed (not locked), bring both dumbbells straight up to the sides, until they are just above shoulder height (exhale). *(Illus. B)*

2. Pause briefly, then slowly lower dumbbells to starting position (inhale).

3. Repeat for desired number of reps.

Note Don't bend your wrists.

B

A

Variations
A. One-Arm Side Lateral: Raise one arm at a time, alternating arms until you've done the correct number of reps with each arm. Don't lean to the side.

B. Standing Side Lateral: Stand, holding dumbbells together in front of your thighs. Do exercise as above, both arms at once or alternating.

C. Leaning Side Lateral: Grasp onto a sturdy fixture such as the edge of a kitchen sink or the knob of a closed door, and lean out at arm's length. Do one full set with one arm, then switch arms.

D. Lying Side Lateral: Lie on your left side, legs crossed. Hold the dumbbell in your right hand, palm facing down, arm extended. Raise dumbbell until directly above right shoulder. Pause, lower slowly to starting position. Complete one full set, then switch sides.

Front Shoulder Raise
(works front of shoulder)

Starting Position Stand with weights held in front of your thighs, arms straight, elbows relaxed, palms facing thighs. *(Illus. A)*

Movement
1. Raise one arm slightly higher than shoulder height (exhale). *(Illus. B)*
2. Pause, then lower slowly to starting position (inhale).
3. Repeat with other arm. Do prescribed number of reps with each arm.

Notes
• Keep wrists straight.
• Don't arch your back.

B

A

• Try to keep your trunk motionless; if you can't help swinging your body you're probably using too much weight.

Variations
A. Above-the-Head Front Shoulder Raise: Instead of stopping at shoulder height, bring the dumbbells straight up over your head, pause, then return to starting position.
B. Seated Front Shoulder Raise: Sit with feet firmly on the floor, dumbbells at your sides. Perform exercise as above.
C. Hammer Front Shoulder Raise: Palms face each other; otherwise perform just as above.

Reverse Fly
(works rear shoulder)

Starting Position   Sit on a chair or bench, leaning forward, knees together, on the balls of your feet. Hold the dumbbells together in front of your shins. *(Illus. A)*

Movement
1. Raise the dumbbells out to your sides in a circular motion, to shoulder height (exhale). *(Illus. B)*

2. Pause, then lower dumbbells to starting position (inhale).

3. Repeat for desired number of reps.

Notes
• If it feels more comfortable for you, start with the dumbbells behind instead of in front of your calves.

• Lean forward so chest is as close as possible to thighs (to protect your back).

A

B

Exercises for Biceps

(front of upper arm)

Regular Curl

Starting Position Stand with your knees relaxed, pelvis tucked, shoulders dropped, chin level, feet approximately shoulder width apart. Hold a dumbbell in each hand, arms extended straight down from the shoulders, palms forward. *(Illus. A)*

Movement
1. Bending the elbow, exhale as you bring one dumbbell up about ¾ of the way towards your shoulder. *(Illus. B)*
2. Inhale as you return to starting position.
3. Repeat with other arm, and continue alternating arms, performing the desired number of repetitions with each arm.

Notes
• *Don't bend your wrists*.
• To get maximum benefit, lift the weight only to the point of "peak contraction." You will know when you have gone beyond that point, because the lifting suddenly gets easier.
• Don't swing the dumbbells; strive for a controlled, even movement.
• Keep your elbows close to your body.

Variations
A. As you become stronger, try doing curls with both arms at once, or use a barbell if you have one.
B. Seated Curl: Done sitting down, the dumbbells will be suspended at your sides. Seated curls are more difficult; try them only after you've become comfortable with regular (standing) curls.

A

B

Concentration Curl

Starting Position Sit on the edge of a chair, both feet firmly on the floor, knees open wide. With your right hand, hold a dumbbell between your legs at arm's length, with the back of the upper right arm resting against the inner right thigh near the knee. You will be leaning slightly forward. *(Illus. A)*

Movement
1. Curl the dumbbell up by bending your elbow, until the dumbbell is ¾ of the way to your shoulder (exhale). *(Illus. B)*
2. Slowly lower the weight to starting position (inhale).
3. Repeat for prescribed number of reps.
4. Reverse position and repeat steps 1 through 3 with left arm.

Notes
• Don't bend your wrist.
• Keep the arm pressed against the inner thigh, making sure the upper arm is always vertical.

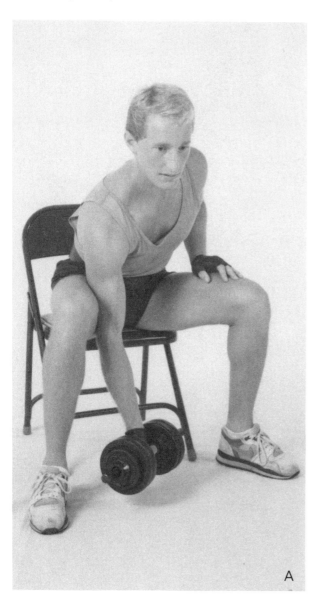

A

B

Hammer Curl

Starting Position Stand with your knees relaxed, pelvis tucked, shoulders dropped, chin level, feet approximately shoulder width apart. Hold a dumbbell in each hand, arms extended straight down at your sides, *palms facing toward you* (this is how it differs from Regular Curls). *(Illus. A)*

Movement

1. Bending at the elbow, curl one dumbbell up about ¾ of the way to your shoulder (exhale). *(Illus. B)*

2. Return to starting position (inhale).

3. Repeat with the other arm, and continue alternating arms, performing desired number of reps with each arm.

Notes

- Lift the weight only to the point of "peak contraction" (see second note under Regular Curl).
- Don't swing the dumbbells.
- Keep elbows close to your body.

Variations

A. As you become stronger, you can try doing curls with both arms at once.

B. Seated Hammer Curl: Done sitting down, the dumbbells will be suspended at your sides. Seated curls are more difficult; try them only after you've become comfortable with standing curls.

C. Hammer Curl with a Twist: Starting position is the same as the basic exercise. As you bring the dumbbell up, turn it gradually so that the palm is facing up (towards the body at the top of the movement). As you lower the dumbbell, turn it gradually back to starting position (palm facing in).

A

B

Side Curl

Starting Position Stand with your knees relaxed, pelvis tucked, shoulders dropped, chin level, feet approximately shoulder width apart. Hold a dumbbell in each hand, arms extended straight down at your sides, *palms facing out. (Illus. A)*

Movement
1. Bending at the elbow, curl one dumbbell up to the side about ¾ of the way toward your shoulder (exhale). *(Illus. B)*
2. Return to starting position (inhale).
3. Repeat with other arm. Continue alternating arms, performing correct number of repetitions with each arm.

Notes
• Lift the weight only to the point of "peak contraction" (see note under Regular Curl).
• Keep upper arm and elbow pressed into your side.
• Keep wrists straight.
• Do not lean to the side; hold your body erect during the entire exercise.

Variations
A. As you become stronger, you can try doing curls with both arms at once.
B. This exercise can also be done sitting down. For the Seated Side Curl the dumbbells will be suspended at your sides. Doing curls while seated is more difficult; try them only after you've become comfortable with standing curls.

A

B

Extended Side Curl

Starting Position   Sit on the floor by the side of a chair. Rest the back of your right upper arm and elbow on the seat of the chair. Hold a dumbbell in your hand, arm extended. *(Illus. A)*

Movement

1. Bending at the elbow, curl the dumbbell up halfway to the shoulder, until your forearm is vertical (exhale). *(Illus. B)*

2. Return slowly to starting position (inhale).
3. Repeat for prescribed number of reps.
4. Repeat steps 1 through 3 with left arm.

Notes
• Keep wrist straight.
• If you don't have a suitable chair (without arms), use a table, the back of a couch, a chest, or whatever you can find. Adjust your position so that your upper arm is horizontal. You can use a folded towel to prop up your elbow.

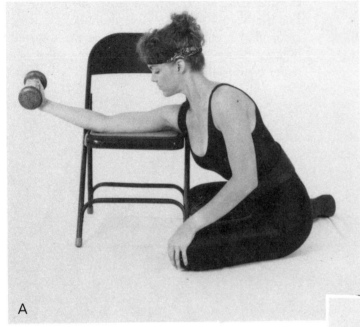

A

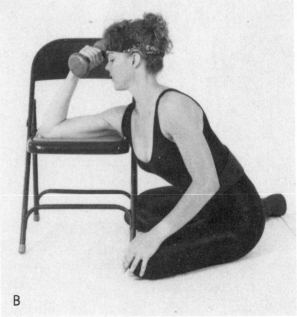

B

Preacher Curl

Starting Position   Sit on the floor, knees bent. Rest the back of your right arm, just above the elbow, on your knee. Use a folded towel in between knee and arm as padding. Hold a dumbbell in your right hand, arm extended. Place your left hand on the floor for support. Your feet should be far enough away from your body so that the upper arm points at an angle toward the floor. *(Illus. A)* If you happen to have an adjustable (incline) bench, you can lean over the top of it and use the bench to support your arm.

Movement
1. Bending at the elbow, curl the dumbbell up about ¾ of the way toward your shoulder (exhale). *(Illus. B)*
2. Return to starting position (inhale).
3. Repeat for prescribed number of reps.
4. Reverse position and repeat with left arm. Continue alternating arms, performing desired number of sets with each arm.

Notes
• Lift the weight only to the point of "peak contraction" (see note under Regular Curl).
• When your arm is in the fully extended position, make sure your elbow is not locked.
• Keep your wrist straight.

A

B

Exercises for Triceps

(back of the upper arm)

Overhead Extension

Starting Position Sit on the edge of a chair, bench or stool. Hold a single dumbbell over your head with both hands, palms up and thumbs wrapped around the handle. Keep upper arms close to your head. Your arms should be extended, but do not lock your elbows. *(Illus. A)*

Movement

1. Inhale as you bend your arms at the elbows, so that the dumbbell is slowly lowered behind your neck. *(Illus. B)*

2. Exhale as you straighten your arms and lift the dumbbell to starting position.

3. Repeat for desired number of reps.

Notes
• Keep your chin level.
• Do not arch your back.

Variation One-Arm Overhead Extension: Grip the dumbbell in the normal fashion (by the handle), with one hand only. Point your elbow toward the ceiling, arm close to head. Use the other hand to support the arm that you're working. Repeat above instructions, performing an entire set before changing arms.

A

B

Kickback

Starting Position   Lean over a chair, resting one hand on the seat, holding a dumbbell in the other hand. Make sure your back is not arched. Lift your upper arm so it is parallel to the floor, keeping lower arm vertical. *(Illus. A)*

Movement

1. Press the dumbbell back until the entire arm is parallel to the floor (exhale). *(Illus. B)*
2. Hold briefly, return to starting position (inhale).

3. Repeat for prescribed number of reps, then switch arms and continue alternating arms, doing the correct number of sets with each arm.

Notes

• Keep your elbow lifted and close to your body.
• Don't swing the dumbbell and let momentum do the work for you. Go slowly and feel those muscles work!
• Don't lock the elbow of the arm you're leaning on.

Straight-Arm Kickback

This exercise is excellent for tightening the very top portion of the back of the arm.

Starting Position   Lean over a chair, resting one hand on the seat, holding a dumbbell in the other hand. Relax both elbows (do not lock them). Make sure your back is not arched. The arm holding the dumbbell is extended down toward the floor. *(Illus. A)*

Movement

1. Keeping your arm straight, raise the dumbbell back until your entire arm is parallel to the floor (exhale). *(Illus. B)*

2. Hold briefly, return to starting position (inhale).

3. Repeat for prescribed number of reps, then switch arms and continue alternating arms, doing the correct number of sets with each arm.

Note   Don't swing the weight. Especially, avoid going too far forward as you're bringing the dumbbell back to its starting position.

Combination Kickback

This is a combination of the previous two exercises.

Starting Position   Lean over a chair, resting one hand on the seat, holding a dumbbell in the other hand. Relax both elbows. Make sure your back is not arched. The arm holding the dumbbell is extended down. *(Illus. A)*

Movement

1. Raise the dumbbell back until your entire arm is parallel to the floor (exhale). *(Illus. B)*

2. Keeping the upper arm straight back, bend your elbow so that the forearm is vertical (inhale). *(Illus. C)*

3. Press the dumbbell back until the entire arm is again parallel to the floor (exhale). *(Illus. D)*

4. Return to starting position, entire arm vertical (inhale).

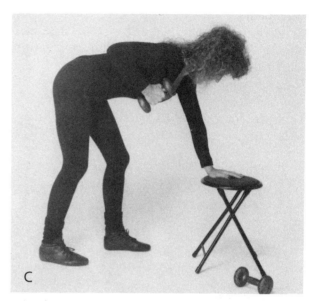

C

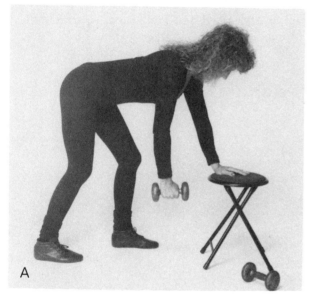

A

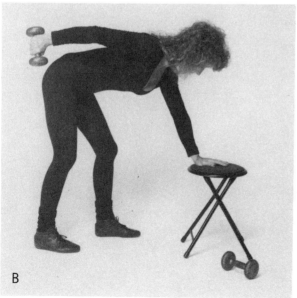

D

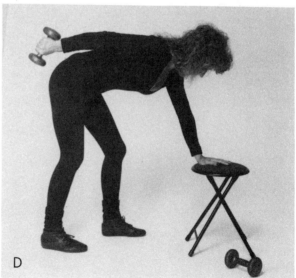

B

5. Repeat steps 1 through 4 for prescribed number of reps, then switch arms and repeat.

Note   Don't swing the dumbbell. Especially, avoid going too far forward as you're bringing the dumbbell back to its starting position.

Black Eye

Starting Position   Lie on your back on the floor with your knees bent. Hold the dumbbell in your left hand, arm extended toward the ceiling. Use your right arm to support your left arm, midway between the shoulder and the elbow. Do not lock the left elbow. *(Illus. A)*

Movement

1. Slowly lower the dumbbell to your shoulder, keeping the elbow pointed toward the ceiling (inhale). *(Illus. B)*
2. Bring the dumbbell back up to starting position (exhale).
3. Repeat for prescribed number of reps, then switch arms and repeat.

Note   Bring the dumbbell down slowly. (For maximum weight training benefit, you should always lower the weight slowly in any exercise. Here, it is especially important because of the risk of losing control of the dumbbell and dropping it on yourself.)

Variation   This exercise can also be done with both arms at once. Hold a single dumbbell (one hand on each end), or a barbell (hands fairly close together on the bar), and lower it to just above your forehead. As you gain confidence and strength, you can try this variation with a dumbbell in each hand, lowering them to your shoulders as in the original description above.

A

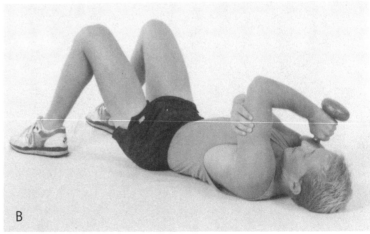

B

Dip

Starting Position Grab the near edge of a sturdy chair or bench positioned behind you, and lean with your legs extended so that your weight is distributed between your heels and your hands. *(Illus. A)*

Movement
1. Bending your elbows, slowly lower your body until your upper arms are parallel to the floor (inhale). *(Illus. B)*
2. Push yourself back up to starting position (exhale).
3. Repeat as many times as you can.

Notes
• Keep your back straight.
• Don't lock your elbows.

Variation To make the exercise harder, elevate your feet.

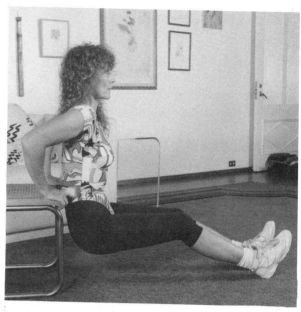

The Dip can be done without gym equipment by making use of household furniture.

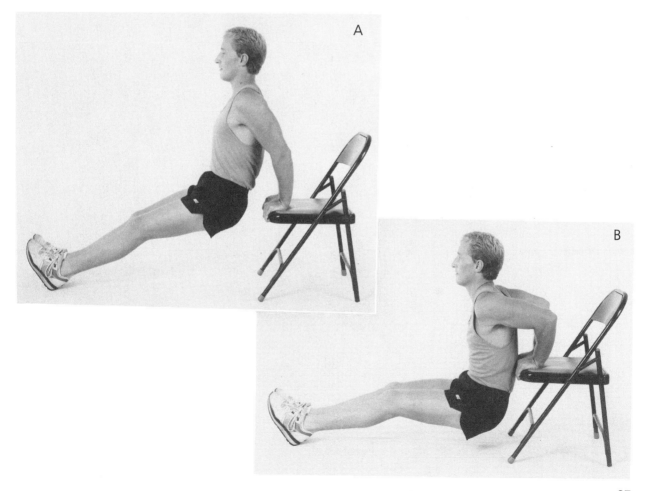

Abdominal Exercises

When most people think of abdominal (stomach) exercises, they think of sit-ups. However, traditional sit-ups put undue strain on the lower back and only work the middle portion of the abdominal muscles. The exercises here will work the entire abdominal region while sparing your spine. A good abdominal exercise program is important for posture and to prevent or reduce lower-back problems.

In order to get the best from your workouts, follow these general rules:

• Instead of doing 3 or 4 sets of 8–12 repetitions, as with most of the other exercises, we recommend that you do only one set of each abdominal exercise, but do as many reps as you can.
• Except for standing exercises and those which use the legs in the performance of the exercise, always keep your knees bent (pointed toward the ceiling) while working the "abs."
• Try to keep your abdominal muscles pulled in (contracted) at all times while doing the exercises.

A

B

Twist
(works obliques — muscles at side of waist — and lower back)

Starting Position   Stand with your feet parallel, about shoulder width apart, knees straight but not locked, pelvis tucked, neck straight. Hold a light pair of dumbbells (8 pounds maximum) halfway between your shoulders and neck, one on each side of your neck. *(Illus. A)*

Movement
1. Keeping your hips squared towards the front, twist from the waist, allowing your entire torso, neck, and head to follow. *(Illus. B)*
2. Twist to the other side.
3. Repeat 20 to 50 times.

Notes
• This is a continuous-movement exercise. Do not pause at the front.
• Remember to keep your hips squared towards the front. Try not to allow them to twist at all.

Side Bend

(works the obliques—muscles at side of waist)

Starting Position   Stand with your feet parallel, about shoulder width apart, knees straight but not locked. Hold a dumbbell in your right hand at your side. Place your left hand behind your head. *(Illus. A)*

A

B

Movement

1. Keeping the right arm perfectly straight, and bending at the waist, inhale as you lower the dumbbell as close as you can to the floor. *(Illus. B)*

2. Exhale as you return to starting position.

3. Repeat 20 to 50 times, then switch sides and repeat.

Notes

• Don't bend the elbow of the arm holding the dumbbell.

• Keep your neck straight at all times.

Center Curl-Up
(works main abdominal muscles)

Starting Position   Lie on your back on a comfortable surface (one that cushions your spine). Place your right hand behind your head. With your left hand, cradle a dumbbell against your upper chest. Bend your knees up, press your lower back against the floor, tighten your abdominals, and hold your chin up.

Movement
1. Slowly lift your shoulders and upper back off the floor as far as you can, bringing your right elbow towards your knees (exhale). *(Illus. A)*
2. Hold briefly, then curl down slowly (inhale).
3. Repeat as many times as you can.

Notes
• For variety and balance, do the exercise sometimes with the right hand holding the dumbbell.
• Don't arch your back; as much as possible keep your lower back pressed to the floor.

A

Side Curl-Up
(works main abdominals and obliques)

Starting Position   Lie on your back on a comfortable surface (one that cushions your spine). Place your left hand behind your head. With your right hand, cradle a dumbbell midway between your chest and left shoulder. Place the back of your right ankle on top of your left knee.

Movement
1. Exhale as you lift your shoulders and upper back as high as you can, pressing the left elbow towards the right knee (attempt to touch the elbow to the knee). *(Illus. B)*
2. Inhale as you slowly curl down to starting position.
3. Repeat as many times as you can.
4. Reverse position and repeat steps 1 through 3, curling right elbow toward left knee.

Notes
• Elbow of arm holding head should not open and close; keep your elbow pointed up throughout the movement.
• Keep your neck straight; avoid the tendency to roll your head forward on the upward movement.
• Try to keep your abdominals contracted. As the muscles get stronger, this will become easier.
• Don't arch your back.

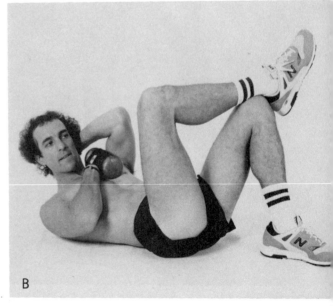

B

Abdominal Crunch—Center
(works upper part of abdominals)

Starting Position   Lie on your back on a comfortable surface (one that cushions your spine). Place one hand behind your head. With the other hand, cradle a dumbbell against your upper chest. Bend your knees up, press your lower back against the floor, and tighten your stomach. Lift your shoulders and upper back slightly off the floor.

Movement
1. Press your shoulders a little higher in short, pulsing movements, exhaling each time as you press up. *(Illus. A)*
2. Continue for as many reps as you can, without lowering the shoulders to the floor until you're done.

Notes
• Keep your neck straight; avoid the tendency to roll your head forward on the upward movement.
• Keep the abdominal muscles contracted (tight).

Abdominal Crunch—Side
(works upper and outer portion of abdominals)

Starting Position   Lie on your back on a comfortable surface (one that cushions your spine). Place your left hand behind your head. With your right hand, cradle a dumbbell midway between your chest and left shoulder. Place the back of your right ankle on top of your left knee. Lift your shoulders and upper back slightly off the floor.

Movement
1. Pulse the left elbow towards the right knee. Do not attempt to touch elbow to knee at first. Exhale with each upward pulse. *(Illus. B)*
2. Continue for as many reps as you can, without lowering the shoulders to the floor until you're done.
3. Reverse position and repeat (right elbow to left knee).

Notes
• Keep your neck straight; avoid the tendency to roll your head forward on the upward movement.
• Keep the abdominal muscles contracted (tight).

A

B

Ab Curl/Leg Lift
(works entire abdominal region)

Starting Position   Lie on your back on a comfortable surface (one that cushions your spine). Bend your right knee up and place your right foot flat on the floor. Extend your left leg on the floor, foot flexed. Place your right hand behind your head. With the left hand cradle a dumbbell against your upper chest.

Movement

1. Curl your shoulders up as you lift your left leg straight up toward the ceiling (exhale). *(See illustration)*

2. Slowly lower your leg and shoulders to the floor.

3. Repeat for 15 to 20 repetitions.

4. Point your left foot, repeat steps 1 through 3 with foot pointed.

5. Bring your left leg out to the side as far as you can without bending it, flex foot and repeat steps 1 through 3. Keep your left knee and foot rotated out, so that you're lifting with the inner thigh. Press the right elbow towards the left knee as you curl up.

6. Point your left foot and repeat step 5.

7. Change legs and arms, repeat steps 1 through 6.

Notes
- Keep your neck straight; don't roll your head forward on the upward movement.
- Strive for a slow, controlled movement; don't rely on momentum.

Half Sit-Up

(works upper and middle portions of abdominal muscles)

CAUTION: This is an advanced exercise which puts stress on the lower back. It should *only* be done after conditioning your body for several months with the other exercises in this book.

Starting Position Sit on the floor. Hook your feet under a couch, bed, or heavy piece of furniture. Make sure the floor under your lower back and tailbone is well padded. Clasp your hands behind your head.

Movement

1. Lower your torso ½ to ⅔ of the way to the floor, squeezing your abdominal muscles (inhale). *(See illustrations below)*

2. Return to sitting position, bringing your elbows towards your knees (exhale). Try not to come all the way up; stop while you still feel some tension in your stomach muscles.

3. Repeat as many times as you can.

Note If you feel any lower-back pain or discomfort, **stop immediately**.

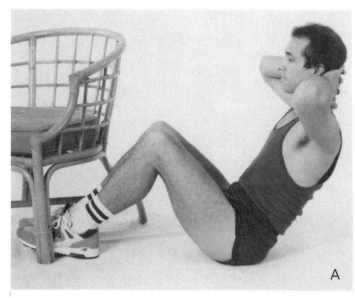

A

B

Leg Extension
(works lower part of abdominals)

CAUTION: If you have lower-back problems, avoid this exercise.

Starting Position   Lie on your back on a comfortable surface (one that cushions your spine). Interlace your hands behind your head. Cross your ankles, knees open and pulled to your chest. *(Illus. A)*

Movement

1. Extend your legs out as you press your knees together (exhale). *(Illus. B)*
2. Return to starting position (inhale).
3. Repeat 15 to 20 times.
4. Roll slightly to the right, shifting your weight to the right hip, then repeat steps 1 through 3.

5. Shift your weight to the left hip; do another 15 to 20 reps.

Notes

• If this exercise hurts your lower back or tailbone, place your fists under the small of your back and tilt your tailbone up. Or, to alleviate pressure on the tailbone, skip steps 1 through 3 and just do steps 4 and 5.
• The higher you extend your legs (the greater the angle from the floor), the easier the exercise becomes. As you gain strength, extend your legs closer to the floor.

Variation   Clasp a dumbbell between your two feet if you would like to give yourself a greater challenge.

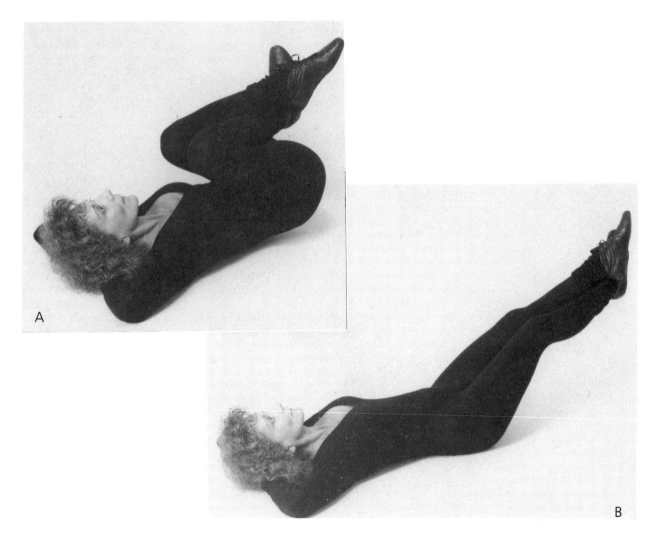

A

B

Knee-Up
(works inner and lower parts of abdominals)

Starting Position   Lie on your back on a comfortable surface. Interlace your hands behind your head. Cross your ankles, pull your knees to your chest as close as you can. *(Illus. A)*

Movement

1. *Without* opening and closing your knees, curl your tailbone off the floor as high as you can (exhale). *(Illus. B)*

2. Hold briefly, then slowly curl tailbone back down (inhale).

3. Hold momentarily then repeat, as many times as you can.

Note   To avoid using momentum and decreasing the benefits of the exercise, be sure to pause briefly at both the top and bottom of the movement.

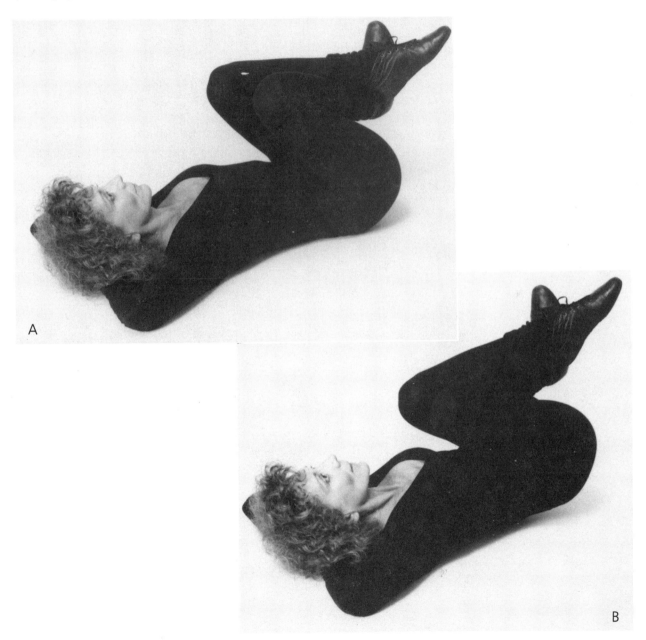

A

B

Tailbone Lift
(works inner and lower parts of abdominals)

Starting Position   Lie on your back on a comfortable surface. Interlace your hands behind your head. Cross your ankles, and point your legs straight up towards the ceiling.

Movement
1. Keeping your legs vertical, lift your tailbone as high as you can (exhale). *(See illustration)*
2. Hold for 2 seconds.
3. Slowly lower tailbone (inhale).
4. Repeat as many times as you can.

Note   Keep your legs perpendicular to the floor; do not let them come towards your head.

Walking in Place
(works lower parts of abdominals)

Starting Position   Lie on your back on a comfortable surface. Interlace your hands behind your head. Bend your knees so your feet are flat on the floor.

Movement

1. Bring your right elbow and your left knee towards each other as close as you can, trying to touch them together (exhale). *(See illustration)*

2. Return to starting position (inhale).
3. Bring your left elbow and your right knee towards each other as close as you can, trying to touch them together (exhale).
4. Return to starting position (inhale).
5. Repeat steps 1 through 4 as many times as you can.

Note   Don't push your head forward on the upward movement; let it rest in your hands with your neck relatively straight.

Calf Exercises

Seated Calf Raise

Starting Position   Sit on a chair, with a small stool, a dictionary, or a stack of hardback books in front of you, or face a stair. Place the balls of your feet on the edge of the stool, books, or stair, feet parallel. Hold the dumbbells so they are resting on your legs a few inches above the knees. Make sure your chair is positioned so that your knees are directly over your ankles.

Movement
1. Keeping the balls of your feet in place, lift your heels up as high as you're able (exhale). *(Illus. A)*
2. Slowly lower your heels down as far as you can (inhale). *(Illus. B)*
3. Repeat for desired number of reps.

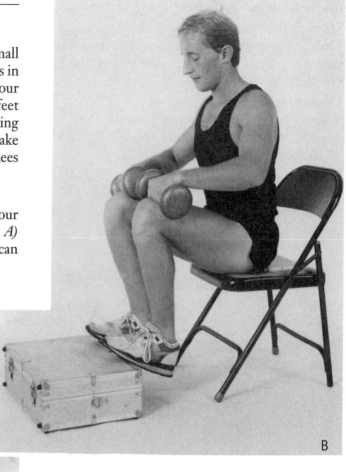

B

A

4. Rest a minute, then for your second set, turn your toes inward, stand "pigeon-toed," and repeat steps 1 through 3.
5. For your third set, turn your toes out, in a V shape, and repeat the exercise.

Note   Maintain a slow, controlled movement, both going up and going down.

Standing Calf Raise

Starting Position   Stand with the ball of your left foot on the edge of a step, a heavy dictionary, or a low, sturdy stool braced against a wall. (A stair is ideal for this one; the object must be very stable.) Wrap your right foot around the back of your left ankle. Hold a dumbbell in your left hand, arm relaxed at your side. Use your right hand for balance.

Movement
1. Keeping the ball of your foot in place, lift your left heel up as high as you're able (exhale). *(Illus. A)*

2. Slowly lower your heel down as far as you can (inhale). *(Illus. B)*
3. Repeat for desired number of reps.
4. Switch dumbbell to right hand and repeat steps 1 through 3 with right foot.

Notes
• Maintain a slow, controlled movement, both going up and going down.
• Keep your hips stable; don't move them back and forth.
• If at first this exercise is too difficult for you, try it without the dumbbell. If still not possible, do it with both legs at once, so as to put only half the burden on each foot, or stick with Seated Calf Raises until you develop more calf strength.

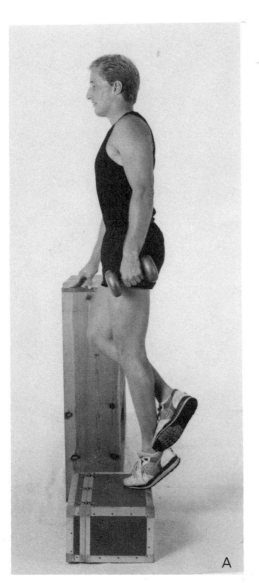

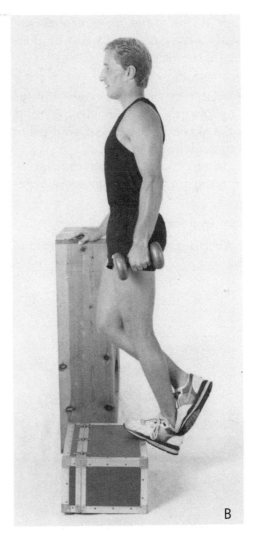

Exercises for Forearms and Wrists

Don't skip these exercises completely, even though they seem less important. The wrists and forearms are often the weak links in your body, limiting the exercises you can do for major muscle groups. By strengthening your wrists and forearms with the exercises in this section, you'll do better at the chest, back, shoulder, biceps, and triceps exercises.

Reverse Curl
(works forearms)

Starting Position Stand with feet shoulder width apart, knees relaxed, pelvis tucked, shoulders dropped, chin level. Hold the dumbbells in front of your thighs, *palms facing towards your thighs. (Illus. A)* This exercise can also be done with a barbell if you have one.

Movement
1. Bending your arms at the elbows, lift the dumbbells up towards your shoulders (exhale). *(Illus. B)* At the top of the movement, your palms will be facing away from you.
2. Slowly return to starting position (inhale).
3. Repeat for the prescribed number of repetitions.

Note Don't bend your wrists.

Variation Alternate arms if you like, instead of doing both at once.

A

B

Side Reverse Curl
(works forearms)

Starting Position Stand with feet shoulder width apart, knees relaxed, pelvis tucked, shoulders dropped, chin level. Hold the dumbbells at your sides, palms facing in towards you. *(Illus. A)*

Movement

1. Bending your arms at the elbows, lift the dumbbells up to the sides toward your shoulders (exhale). *(Illus. B)*

2. Slowly return to starting position (inhale).

3. Perform the prescribed number of repetitions.

Note Don't bend your wrists.

Variation Alternate arms if you like, instead of doing both at once.

Forward Wrist Curl

(works the wrists)

Starting Position   Sit in a chair, resting your forearms on your thighs so that your wrists are on top of your knees, palms facing up. Hold a dumbbell in each hand. This exercise can also be done with a barbell if you have one.

Movement

1. Roll both your wrists up as high as you can (exhale). *(Illus. A)*
2. Lower the dumbbells so that the backs of your fists touch the fronts of your knees (inhale). *(Illus. B)*
3. Perform the prescribed number of repetitions.

Variations

A. Alternate wrists if you like.
B. Standing Forward Wrist Curl: Stand with feet shoulder width apart, knees relaxed, pelvis tucked, shoulders dropped, chin level. Hold dumbbells with your arms hanging at your sides, palms facing forward. Roll your wrists up to the front as far as you can, then down and up to the back as far as you can. (You will need to use lighter dumbbells with this variation.)

A

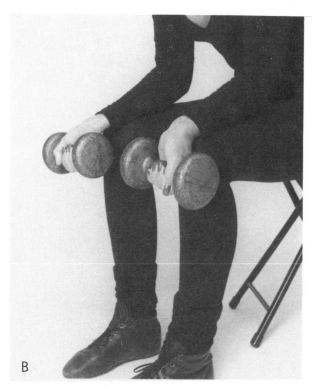

B

Reverse Wrist Curl

(works the wrists)

Starting Position Sit in a chair, resting your forearms on your thighs so that the wrists are on top of your knees, palms facing down. Hold a dumbbell in each hand (or use a barbell).

Movement

1. Roll both wrists up as high as you can (exhale). *(Illus. A)*
2. Lower the dumbbells so that your knuckles touch the fronts of your knees (inhale). *(Illus. B)*
3. Perform the desired number of repetitions.

Variations

A. Alternate wrists if you like.
B. Standing Reverse Wrist Curls: Stand with feet shoulder width apart, knees relaxed, pelvis tucked, shoulders dropped, chin level. Hold dumbbells with your arms hanging at your sides, palms facing back. Roll your wrists up to the front as far as you are able, then down and up to the back as far as you can. (You will need to use lighter dumbbells when performing this variation.)

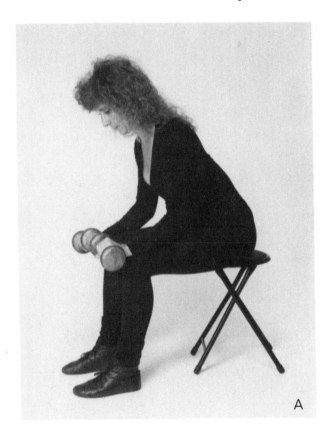

A

B

Workout Programs

The instructions for the following programs are as complete as possible. However, there are certain things you must do for yourself (aside from lifting the weights!). The most important thing is to decide how much weight to use for each exercise. The first time around, the only way to do this is by trial and error. Err on the light side; start with 3 to 5 pound dumbbells for women and 5 to 10 pounders for men (depending on the type of exercise and your prior condition). Try a few reps with that weight and see how it feels. Adjust your weight up or down as necessary. Choose a weight with which you can get through your first set without any real difficulty. The amount of this weight will vary depending on the type of exercise.

After you've been on a program for a while, you'll find it getting easier. You can tell you need to add weight when an exercise becomes so easy that, at the end of the last set, you don't feel as if you've done anything. Allow yourself to progress slowly; if you started with 3-pound dumbbells move up to 5-pounders on that exercise, then 8, then 10. Men can generally progress (with caution) in 5-pound increments.

If your goal is to add muscle mass rather than just toning and shaping, then you need to use enough weight so that your muscles are regularly worked to failure. Muscle failure occurs when you cannot complete even one more repetition of an exercise — in true bodybuilding it is more important to reach this state than it is to complete the prescribed number of repetitions.

The programs are organized by levels of difficulty, as follows:

Level One: Beginner programs
Level Two: Advanced Beginner programs
Level Three: Intermediate programs
Level Four: Advanced programs

If you are working out regularly three or four times a week, you should generally work out at each level for at least two months before moving up to the next level. Do two programs from each level before advancing to the next level, sticking with each program for about four weeks.

The basic programs are organized according to their level. Following the basic programs, we have included some specialty programs: those emphasizing the lower body (legs, buttocks, and hips); programs emphasizing the upper body; and "circuit programs." Circuit programs are quick workouts that will help achieve general fitness and some strengthening and toning benefits. As with anything else, how much you get out of weight training depends on how much you put in. Despite the inflated claims of some fitness programs that promise miraculous results in twenty minutes a day or less, circuit-type programs are not as effective in truly reshaping your body. If that is your goal, make the time for the regular, full-length programs. Although your workouts may be difficult at first, you will soon come to enjoy the exertion, the sense of accomplishment, and the visible results that go with a conscientious workout program.

Many of the programs in the following chapters are designed as "split" programs; that is, you do half of the program on days 1 and 3 of your workout week and half on days 2 and 4. With this schedule, you should work out four times per week. If you prefer, you can do the whole program each time in a single session. In that case, it will take you longer, of course, but you need only work out three times per week instead of four.

Each program contains suggested warm-up exercises and cool-down stretches. Don't feel that you need to stick to the ones mentioned. As a warm-up, any exercise that gets your heart rate up and your blood flowing to the muscles (jogging in place, jumping jacks, riding a stationary bicycle, etc.) will do. Do try to pick warm-up exercises that use the muscles you intend to work

on that day. Many of the programs have the abdominal exercises at the beginning, since abdominal exercises provide an additional warm-up. If you like, you may do them first even when they are designated later in the program.

Don't feel that you have to follow the programs exactly. Once you're familiar with the basic principles of weight training discussed in this book, you can make minor changes for convenience without hurting your workout progress. For example, if a program says to do 3 sets of 8 reps of a given exercise, and you've progressed to

Working out with a friend is a good way to stay on your program.

the point where 8 reps is too easy but you're not quite ready to move up to the next size dumbbells, then go ahead and do 10 or 12 reps per set. This way, you'll continue to progress, and in a week or two you'll be ready to use heavier weights and go back to 8 reps.

If you'd like to make up some of your own programs, follow the guidelines in chapter 9, beginning on page 147. If you're interested in specialized weight training to increase your skill at a particular sport, refer to the section on "Specificity Training," page 150, for some programs tailored to specific sports.

Finally, you'll note that the programs that follow are all based on a dumbbell workout, which is as effective as any method and is for most people the easiest and most convenient home workout. However, in case you have a barbell and bench set, or a commercial "home gym," we've included a few options using that equipment. If you're using dumbbells, just ignore those notes.

THE PROGRAMS	PAGE

Level One Programs

As with most of the programs in this book, the following are designed to be done in either of two ways: you can do the whole program in a single session, or split it as indicated into two workouts, one to be done on the first and third days you work out, and the other on the second and fourth days. Abdominal exercises can be done every day that you work out, or you can save them for days 2 and 4 if you prefer. (Note that the days do not need to be consecutive; for example, with a Monday, Wednesday, Friday, and Saturday schedule, you would do part one on Monday and Friday and part two on Wednesday and Saturday.) If you choose to do the whole program in a single, longer workout session, you need only do it three times a week. For the lower-body (thighs and buttocks) exercises on Level One, start by doing them without any weights, then add light dumbbells when you feel ready. This is also a good idea for the single lower-back exercise in each of the Level One programs, as noted below.

PROGRAM 1
(level one)

Days 1 & 3

SUGGESTED WARM-UPS

Neck — **Turn** (page 25)
Shoulders and Arms — **Roll** (page 26)
Chest and Back — **Arm Raise to Front** (page 27)
Torso — **Twist** (page 29)
Lower Back — **Roll-Down** (page 31)
Legs — **Standing Leg Extension** (page 32)
Hips — **Swing** (page 34)
Ankles — **Roll** (page 35)
Calves — **Lift** (page 36)

LOWER BODY

Start *without weights* for Level One leg exercises.

Standing Exercises

Standard Squat
(pages 52–53)
2 sets, 15 reps
(2 sets, 15 repetitions per set)

Floor Exercises

Pelvic Tilt
(page 65)
1 set, 25 reps

BACK

Good Morning
(page 67)
2 sets, 10 reps
No weights at first.

Bent-Over Row
(page 71)
2 sets, 10 reps

CHEST

Dumbbell Press
(page 77)
2 sets, 10 reps

Pullover
(page 80)
2 sets, 10 reps

ABDOMINALS

Optional on days 1 and 3.

Abdominal Crunch — Center
(page 101)
1 set, as many as you can

Knee-Up
(page 105)
1 set, as many as you can

COOL-DOWN STRETCHES

Perform one stretch for each body part (neck, shoulders, back, lower body, etc).

SUGGESTED WARM-UPS

Neck—**Turn** (page 25)
Shoulders and Arms—**Roll** (page 26)
Chest and Back—**Arm Raise to the Front** (page 27)
Torso—**Twist** (page 29)
Lower Back—**Roll-Down** (page 26)

SHOULDERS

Shoulder Press
(page 81)
2 sets, 10 reps

Side Lateral
(page 83)
2 sets, 10 reps

TRICEPS

Overhead Extension
(page 92)
2 sets, 10 reps

Kickback
(page 93)
2 sets, 10 reps

BICEPS

Regular Curl
(page 86)
2 sets, 10 reps

Side Curl
(page 89)
2 sets, 10 reps

ABDOMINALS

Center Curl-Up
(page 100)
1 set, as many as you can

Walking in Place
(page 107)
1 set, as many as you can

COOL-DOWN STRETCHES

Perform one stretch for each body part.

SUGGESTED WARM-UPS

Neck — **Nod** (page 25)
Shoulders and Arms — **Shrug** (page 26)
Chest and Back — **Arm Raise to the Rear** (page 27)
Torso — **Bent-Arm Twist** (page 29)
Lower Back — **Roll-Down** (page 31)
Legs — **Standing Leg Extension** (page 32)
Hips — **Side Lunge** (page 35)
Ankles — **Roll** (page 26)
Calves — **Lift** (page 36)

LOWER BODY

Start *without weights* for Level One leg exercises.

Standing Exercises

Standard Lunge
(page 56)
2 sets, 15 reps

If you have home gym equipment, add
Hamstring Flexor
(page 66)
2 sets, 10 reps
Use one plate only to start with.

Floor Exercises

Fire Hydrant
(page 60)
1 set, 25 reps

BACK

Good Morning
(page 67)
2 sets, 10 reps
Start without weights.

Upright Row
(page 73)
2 sets, 10 reps

CHEST

Pullover
(page 80)
2 sets, 10 reps

Fly
(page 79)
2 sets, 10 reps

ABDOMINALS

Optional on days 1 and 3.

Side Curl-Up
(page 100)
1 set, as many as you can

Ab Curl/Leg Lift
(page 102)
1 set, 15 each side

COOL-DOWN STRETCHES

Perform one stretch for each body part (neck, shoulders, back, lower body, etc.).

SUGGESTED WARM-UPS

Neck — **Nod** (page 25)
Shoulders and Arms — **Shrug** (page 26)
Chest and Back — **Arm Raise to the Rear** (page 27)
Torso — **Bent-Arm Twist** (page 29)
Lower Back — **Roll-Down** (page 31)

SHOULDERS

Reverse Fly
(page 85)
2 sets, 10 reps

Front Shoulder Raise
(page 84)
2 sets, 10 reps

TRICEPS

Straight-Arm Kickback
(page 94)
2 sets, 10 reps

Overhead Extension
(page 92)
2 sets, 10 reps

BICEPS

Hammer Curl
(page 88)
2 sets, 10 reps

Concentration Curl
(page 87)
2 sets, 10 reps

ABDOMINALS

Abdominal Crunch — Center
(page 101)
1 set each side, as many as you can

Leg Extension
(page 104)
1 set, as many as you can

COOL-DOWN STRETCHES

Perform one stretch for each body part.

SUGGESTED WARM-UPS

Neck—**Turn** (page 25)
Shoulders and Arms—**Arm Swing** (page 26)
Chest and Back—**Arm Raise to the Front** (page 27)
Torso—**Side Bend** (page 30)
Lower Back—**Roll-Down** (page 31)
Legs—**Standing Leg Extension** (page 32)
Hips—**Swing** (page 34)
Ankles—**Roll** (page 35)
Calves—**Lift** (page 36)

ABDOMINALS

Optional on days 1 and 3.

Twist
(page 98)
1 set, 20 to 30 reps

Abdominal Crunch—Side
(page 101)
1 set, as many as you can

LOWER BODY

Start *without weights* for Level One leg exercises.

Standing Exercise

Pole Squat
(page 55)
2 sets, 10 reps

Floor Exercise

Double Leg Curl
(page 66)
2 sets, 10 reps

If you have home gym equipment, substitute **Hamstring Flexor** (page 66)
2 sets, 10 reps
Use only one plate to start.

BACK

Shrug
(page 74)
2 sets, 10 reps

Bent-Over Row, variation B
(page 71)
2 sets, 10 reps

If you have home gym equipment, add **Lat Pull-Down** (page 74)
2 sets, 10 reps

CHEST

Push-Up from the Knees
(page 75)
2 sets, 10 reps

Fly
(page 79)
2 sets, 10 reps

COOL-DOWN STRETCHES

Perform one stretch for each body part (neck, shoulders, back, lower body, etc.).

SUGGESTED WARM-UPS

Neck — **Turn** (page 25)
Shoulders and Arms — **Arm Swing**
(page 26)
Chest and Back — **Arm Raise to the
Front** (page 27)
Torso — **Side Bend** (page 30)
Lower Back — **Roll-Down** (page 31)

SHOULDERS

Front Shoulder Raise
(page 84)
2 sets, 10 reps

Shoulder Press
(page 81)
2 sets, 10 reps

TRICEPS

Combination Kickback
(page 95)
2 sets, 10 reps

This is a combination of two exercises,
so you don't need to do another exercise for the triceps.

BICEPS

Regular Curl
(page 86)
2 sets, 10 reps

Hammer Curl
(page 88)
2 sets, 10 reps

ABDOMINALS

Side Curl-Up
(page 100)
1 set each side, as
many as you can

Knee-Up
(page 105)
1 set, as many as
you can

COOL-DOWN STRETCHES

Perform one stretch for each body part.

Level Two Programs

The Level Two programs are designed as "split" programs; that is, you do half of the program on one day and half on the following day, as you will see below. With this schedule, you should work out four times per week. If you prefer, you can do the whole program in one session. In that case, it will take you longer, but you will only have to work out three times per week.

PROGRAM 4
(level two)

Days 1 & 3

SUGGESTED WARM-UPS

Neck — **Nod** (page 25)
Shoulders and Arms — **Shrug** (page 26)
Chest and Back — **Standing Arch-Curl** (page 28)
Torso — **Turn-Out** (page 30)
Lower Back — **Roll-Down** (page 31)
Legs — **Dip** (page 33)
Hips — **Side Lunge** (page 35)
Ankles — **Roll** (page 35)
Calves — **Lift** (page 36)

ABDOMINALS

Optional on days 1 and 3

Abdominal Crunch — Side
(page 101)
1 set, as many as you can

Ab Curl/Leg Lift
(page 102)
1 set each side, as many as you can

LOWER BODY

Standing Exercises

Side Lunge
(page 57)
3 sets, 10 reps

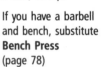

Step-Up
(page 58)
3 sets, 10 reps

If you have home gym equipment, add
Leg Extension
(page 104)
2 sets, 15 reps

Floor Exercise

⅔ Side Leg Lift
(page 63)
1 set, 10 reps, each position

CHEST

Fly
(page 79)
3 sets, 10 reps

Dumbbell Press
(page 77)
3 sets, 10 reps

If you have a barbell and bench, substitute
Bench Press
(page 78)
3 sets, 10 reps

BACK

Shrug
(page 74)
3 sets, 10 reps

Good Morning
(page 67)
3 sets, 10 reps

COOL-DOWN STRETCHES

Perform one stretch for each body part (neck, shoulders, back, lower body, etc.).

SUGGESTED WARM-UPS

Neck — **Nod** (page 25)
Shoulders and Arms — **Shrug** (page 26)
Chest and Back — **Standing Arch-Curl** (page 28)
Torso — **Turn-Out** (page 30)
Lower Back — **Roll-Down** (page 31)

ABDOMINALS

Walking in Place
(page 107)
1 set, as many as
you can

Center Curl-Up
(page 100)
1 set, as many as
you can

SHOULDERS

**Shoulder Press,
variation D,**
(page 81)
3 sets, 10 reps

**Side Lateral,
variation B**
(page 83)
3 sets, 10 reps

TRICEPS

Combination Kickback
(page 95)
2 sets, 10 reps

BICEPS

Preacher Curl
(page 91)
3 sets, 10 reps

COOL-DOWN STRETCHES

Perform one stretch for each body part.

PROGRAM 5
(level two)

Days 1 & 3

SUGGESTED WARM-UPS

Neck — **Turn** (page 25)
Shoulders and Arms — **Arm Swing** (page 26)
Chest and Back — **Arm Raise to the Front** (page 27)
Torso — **Bent-Arm Twist** (page 29)
Lower Back — **Roll-Down** (page 31)
Legs — **Standing Leg Extension** (page 32)
Hips — **Swing** (page 34)
Ankles — **Roll** (page 35)
Calves — **Lift** (page 36)

ABDOMINALS

Optional on days 1 and 3

Side Curl-Up
(page 100)
1 set each side, as many as you can

Walking in Place
(page 107)
1 set, as many as you can

LOWER BODY

Standing Exercises

Wide Turn-Out Squat
(page 54)
3 sets, 10 reps

Standard Lunge
(page 56)
3 sets, 10 reps

If you have home gym equipment, add
Hamstring Flexor
(page 66)
3 sets, 10 reps

Floor Exercise

Quad Lift
(page 64)
3 sets, 10 reps

CHEST

Push-up from the Knees
(page 75)
2 sets, as many reps as you can

Pullover
(page 80)
3 sets, 10 reps

BACK

One-Arm Reverse Fly
(page 72)
3 sets, 10 reps

Straight-Leg Dead Lift
(pages 69–70)
3 sets, 10 reps

COOL-DOWN STRETCHES

Perform one stretch for each body part (neck, shoulders, back, lower body, etc.).

SUGGESTED WARM-UPS

Neck — **Turn** (page 25)
Shoulders and Arms — **Arm Swing**
(page 26)
Chest and Back — **Arm Raise to the Front** (page 27)
Torso — **Bent-Arm Twist** (page 29)
Lower Back — **Roll-Down** (page 31)

ABDOMINALS

Side Bend
(page 99)
1 set, 25 reps each side

Abdominal Crunch — Center
(page 101)
1 set, as many as
you can

SHOULDERS

Arnold Press
(page 82)
3 sets, 10 reps

Front Shoulder Raise, variation C
(page 84)
3 sets, 10 reps

TRICEPS

Black Eye
(page 96)
3 sets, 10 reps

Use a barbell if you have one; see Variation under exercise description.

BICEPS

Extended Side Curl
(page 90)
3 sets, 10 reps

COOL-DOWN STRETCHES

Perform one stretch for each body part.

Level Three Programs

Now that you've advanced to Level Three workouts, you're probably ready to push yourself a little harder. Make sure you use dumbbells heavy enough to really feel it. Adjust the weight you're lifting so that by the last set of each exercise you are working to muscle failure (the point where you can't do even one more repetition no matter how hard you try). When you work out in this way, you will experience more rapid gains. Don't worry if you come up a few reps short in your last set — just give it your best effort! Review the safety rules on page 21, and pay close attention to your form as you do these more advanced workouts.

PROGRAM 6
(level three)

Days 1 & 3

SUGGESTED WARM-UPS

Neck — **Turn** and **Nod** (page 25)
Shoulders and Arms — **Shrug** and **Arm Swing** (page 26)
Chest and Back — **Arm Raise to the Front** and **Arm Raise to the Rear** (page 27)
Torso — **Bent Arm Twist** (page 29) and **Side Bend** (page 30)
Lower Back — **Roll-Down** (page 31)
Legs — **Standing Leg Extension** (page 32) and **Dip** (page 33)
Hips — **Side Lunge** (page 35)
Ankles — **Roll** (page 35)
Calves — **Lift** (page 36)

ABDOMINALS

Optional on days 1 and 3.

Twist
(page 98)
1 set, 50 reps

Abdominal Crunch — Center
(page 101)
2 sets, as many as you can

LOWER BODY

Standing Exercises

Standard Squat
(pages 52–53)
3 sets, 10 reps
Use a barbell if you have one.

Standard Lunge
(page 56)
3 sets, 10 reps
Use a barbell if you have one.

Floor Exercises

Inner Thigh Series
(page 62)
1 set, 10 reps each position

Quad Lift
(page 64)
3 sets, 10 reps

If you have home gym equipment, substitute
Seated Leg Extension
(page 65)
3 sets, 10 reps

CHEST

Push-Up, Standard
(page 76)
or
From the Knees
(page 75)
3 sets, 10 reps

Fly, variation
(page 79)
3 sets, 10 reps

Pullover
(page 80)
3 sets, 10 reps

If you have a bench and barbell, substitute

Bench Press
(page 78)
3 sets, 10 reps

BACK

Straight-Leg Dead Lift
(pages 69–70)
3 sets, 10 reps
Use a barbell if you have one.

Bent-Over Row, variation A
(page 71)
3 sets, 10 reps

Upright Row
(page 73)
3 sets, 10 reps
Use a barbell if you have one.

COOL-DOWN STRETCHES

Perform one stretch for each body part (neck, shoulders, back, lower body, etc.).

SUGGESTED WARM-UPS

Neck — **Turn** and **Nod** (page 25)
Shoulders and Arms — **Shrug** and **Arm Swing** (page 26)
Chest and Back — **Arm Raises to the Front** and **Arm Raises to the Rear** (page 27)
Torso — **Bent Arm Twist** (page 29) and **Side Bend** (page 30)
Lower Back — **Roll-Down** (page 31)

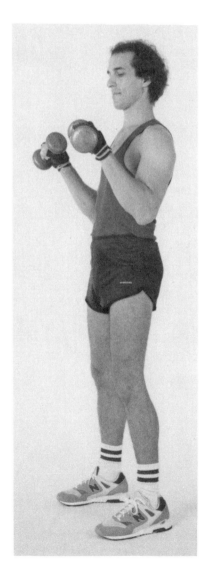

SHOULDERS

Arnold Press
(page 82)
4 sets, 10 reps

Reverse Fly
(page 85)
3 sets, 10 reps

TRICEPS AND BICEPS

Superset (alternate sets of two different exercises — see page 149 for a full explanation of supersetting) as follows:

Overhead Extension, variation
(page 92)
3 sets, 10 reps

superset with

Regular Curl, variation A
(page 86)
3 sets, 10 reps

Combination Kickback
(page 95)
3 sets, 10 reps

superset with

Side Curl, variation A
(page 89)
3 sets, 10 reps

ABDOMINALS

Half Sit-Up
(page 103)
2 sets, as many as you can

Side Curl-Up
(page 100)
1 set each side, as many as you can

Ab Curl/Leg Lift
(page 102)
2 sets, as many as you can

CALVES

Seated Calf Raise
(page 108)
1 set, 10 reps each position

FOREARMS AND WRISTS

Reverse Curl
(page 110)
2 sets, 10 reps
Use a barbell if you have one.

Forward Wrist Curl
(page 112)
2 sets, 10 reps

COOL-DOWN STRETCHES

Perform one stretch for each body part.

SUGGESTED WARM-UPS

Neck — **Turn** and **Nod** (page 25)
Shoulders and Arms — **Roll** and **Shrug** (page 26)
Chest and Back — **Standing Arch-Curl** (page 28)
Torso — **Twist** (page 29) and **Turn-Out** (page 30)
Lower Back — **Roll-Down** (page 31)
Legs — **Dip** (page 33)
Hips — **Swing** (page 34) and **Side Lunge** (page 35)
Ankles — **Roll** (page 26)
Calves — **Lift** (page 36)

ABDOMINALS

Optional on days 1 and 3.

Side Bend
(page 99)
1 set, 50 reps each side

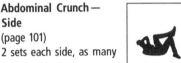

Abdominal Crunch — Side
(page 101)
2 sets each side, as many as you can

LOWER BODY

Standing Exercises

Standard Squat, variation
"Front Squat"
(page 53)
3 sets, 12 reps

Step-Up
(page 58)
3 sets, 12 reps

Floor Exercises

⅔ Side Leg Lift
(page 63)
1 set, 10 reps each position

Pelvic Tilt
(page 65)
1 set, 25 reps

CHEST

Dumbbell Press, variation
(page 77)
3 sets, 10 reps

If you have a bench and barbell, substitute
Bench Press
(page 78)
3 sets, 10 reps

Fly
(page 79)
3 sets, 10 reps

Pullover
(page 80)
3 sets, 10 reps

BACK

Dead Lift
(pages 68–69)
4 sets, 10 reps
Use a barbell if you have one.

Bent-Over Row, variation B
(page 97)
3 sets, 10 reps

COOL-DOWN STRETCHES

Perform one stretch for each body part (neck, shoulders, back, lower body, etc.).

SUGGESTED WARM-UPS

Neck — **Turn** and **Nod** (page 25)
Shoulders and Arms — **Roll** and **Shrug** (page 26)
Chest and Back — **Standing Arch-Curl** (page 28)
Torso — **Twist** (page 29) and **Turn-Out** (page 30)
Lower Back — **Roll-Down** (page 31)

SHOULDERS

Shoulder Press, variation B
(page 81)
3 sets, 10 reps

Front Shoulder Raise, variation A
(page 84)
3 sets, 10 reps

Side Laterals, variation D
(page 83)
3 sets, 10 reps

TRICEPS AND BICEPS

Superset (alternate sets of the two exercises — see page 149 for a full explanation of supersetting) as follows:

Black Eye
(page 96)
3 sets, 10 reps

superset with

Hammer Curl, variation B
(page 88)
3 sets, 10 reps

Dip
(page 97)
3 sets, 10 reps

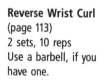

superset with

Extended Side Curl
(page 90)
3 sets, 10 reps

ABDOMINALS

Tailbone Lift
(page 106)
2 sets, as many as you can

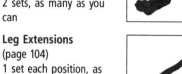

Leg Extensions
(page 104)
1 set each position, as many as you can

Abdominal Crunch — Center
(page 101)
1 set, as many as you can

CALVES

Standing Calf Raise
(page 109)
3 sets, 10 reps

FOREARMS AND WRISTS

Side Reverse Curl
(page 111)
2 sets, 10 reps

Reverse Wrist Curl
(page 113)
2 sets, 10 reps
Use a barbell, if you have one.

COOL-DOWN STRETCHES

Perform one stretch for each body part.

Level Four Programs

If you've advanced to Level Four workouts, you're ready to push yourself a little harder. Make sure you use dumbbells heavy enough that you really feel it. Try to adjust your weight so that by the last set or two of each exercise you are working to muscle failure (the point where you can't do even one more repetition no matter how hard you try). When you work out in this way, you will experience more rapid gains. Don't worry if you come up a few reps short in your last set — just give it your best effort!

Review the safety rules on page 21, and pay close attention to your form as you do these more advanced workouts.

For some Level Four programs emphasizing the upper body, see Programs 14 and 15, on pages 142–144.

The Level Four programs can also be done using the "pyramiding" technique. If you choose to pyramid, ignore the designations below as to sets and reps, and instead follow the instructions and pyramiding formula on page 149.

PROGRAM 8
(level four)

Days 1 & 3

SUGGESTED WARM-UPS

Neck — **Turn** and **Nod** (page 25)
Shoulders and Arms — **Roll** and **Arm Swing** (page 26)
Chest and Back — **Arm Raise to the Front** (page 27) and **Standing Arch-Curl** (page 28)
Torso — **Turn-Out** (page 30) and **Bent-Over Twist** (page 29)
Lower Back — **Roll-Down** (page 31)
Legs — **Standing Leg Extension** (page 32) and **Dip** (page 33)
Hips — **Swing** (page 34) and **Side Lunge** (page 35)
Ankles — **Roll** (page 35)
Calves — **Lift** (page 36)

LOWER BODY

Standing Exercises

Standard Squat variation
(pages 52–53)
3 sets, 8 reps
(Short version:
2 sets, 8 reps)

Step-Up
(page 58)
3 sets, 8 reps
(Short version:
2 sets, 8 reps)

Standard Lunge variation
(page 56)
3 sets, 8 reps
(Short version:
2 sets, 8 reps)
Use a barbell if you have one.

If you're using home gym equipment, substitute
Hamstring Flexor
(page 66)
3 sets, 8 reps

Floor Exercises

⅔ Side Leg Lift
(page 63)
1 set, 10 reps each position

Quad Lift
(page 64)
1 set, 10 reps each position

If you have home gym equipment, substitute
Seated Leg Extension
(page 104)
3 sets, 10 reps

CHEST

Push-Up, Standard
(page 76)
or
From the Knees
(page 75)
3 sets, 8 reps
(Short version:
2 sets, 8 reps)

If you have a bench and barbell, substitute
Bench Press
(page 78)
3 sets, 8 reps

Fly
(page 79)
3 sets, 8 reps
(Short version:
2 sets, 8 reps)

Dumbbell Press, variation
(page 77)
3 sets, 8 reps
(Short version:
2 sets, 8 reps)

BACK

Dead Lift
(pages 68–69)
3 sets, 8 reps
(Short version:
2 sets, 8 reps)
Use a barbell if you have one.

Bent-Over Row, variation B
(page 71)
3 sets, 8 reps
(Short version:
2 sets, 8 reps)

One-Arm Reverse Fly
(page 72)
3 sets, 8 reps
(Short version:
2 sets, 8 reps)

If you have home gym equipment, add
Lat Pull-Down
(page 74) 3 sets, 8 reps

ABDOMINALS

Your choice of 2 of the following exercises each workout, 1 set of as many as you can of each (optional on days 1 and 3):
Center Curl-Up (page 100)
Side Curl-Up (page 100)
Leg Extension (page 104)
Knee-Up (page 105)

COOL-DOWN STRETCHES

Perform two stretches for each body part (neck, shoulders, back, lower body, etc.).

Days 2 & 4

SUGGESTED WARM-UPS

Neck — **Turn** and **Nod** (page 25)
Shoulders and Arms — **Roll** and **Arm Swing** (page 26)
Chest and Back — **Arm Raise to the Front** (page 27) and **Standing Arch-Curl** (page 28)
Torso — **Turn-Out** (page 30) and **Bent-Over Twist** (page 31)
Lower Back — **Roll-Down** (page 31)
Ankles — **Roll** (page 35)
Calves — **Lift** (page 36)

SHOULDERS

Arnold Press
(page 82)
3 sets, 8 reps
(Short version:
2 sets, 8 reps)

Side Lateral, variation C
(page 83)
3 sets, 8 reps
(Short version: 2 sets, 8 reps)

Front Shoulder Raise, variation A
(page 84)
3 sets, 8 reps
(Short version:
2 sets, 8 reps)

TRICEPS

Superset (alternate sets) as follows:

Overhead Extension, variation
(page 92)
3 sets, 10 reps
(Short version:
2 sets, 10 reps)

superset with

Straight-Arm Kickback
(page 94)
3 sets, 10 reps
(Short version:
2 sets, 10 reps)

BICEPS

Superset (alternate sets) as follows:

Hammer Curl, variation C
(page 88)
3 sets, 10 reps
(Short version:
2 sets, 10 reps)

superset with

Concentration Curl
(page 87)
3 sets, 10 reps
(Short version:
2 sets, 10 reps)

ABDOMINALS

Your choice of 2 of the following exercises each workout, 1 set of as many as you can of each:
Center Curl-Up (page 100)
Side Curl-Up (page 100)
Leg Extension (page 104)
Knee-Up (page 105)

CALVES

Standing Calf Raise
(page 109)
3 sets, 8 reps
(Short version:
2 sets, 8 reps)

FOREARMS AND WRISTS

Reverse Curl
(page 110)
1 set, 10 reps

Reverse Wrist Curl
(page 113)
1 set, 10 reps
Use a barbell if you have one.

COOL-DOWN STRETCHES

Perform two stretches for each body part.

SUGGESTED WARM-UPS

Neck — **Turn** and **Nod** (page 25)
Shoulders and Arms — **Roll** and **Shrug** (page 26)
Chest and Back — **Arm Raise to the Rear** (page 27) and **Standing Arch-Curl** (page 28)
Torso — **Bent-Over Twist** (page 31) and **Side Bend** (page 30)
Lower Back — **Roll-Down** (page 31)
Legs — **Standing Leg Extension** (page 32) and **Dip** (page 33)
Hips — **Swing** (page 34) and **Side Lunge** (page 35)
Ankles — **Roll** (page 35)
Calves — **Lift** (page 36)

LOWER BODY

Standing Exercises

Wide Turn-Out Squat
(page 54)
3 sets, 8 reps
(Short version:
2 sets, 8 reps)

Pole Squat
(page 55)
3 sets, 8 reps
(Short version:
2 sets, 8 reps)

If you have home gym equipment, substitute
Seated Leg Extension
(page 65)
3 sets, 8 reps

Side Lunge
(page 57)
3 sets, 8 reps
(Short version:
2 sets, 8 reps)

If you're using home gym equipment, substitute
Hamstring Flexor
(page 66)
3 sets, 8 reps
(Short version:
2 sets, 8 reps)

Floor Exercises

Inner Thigh Series
(page 62)
1 set, 10 reps each position

Knee Lift to the Rear with Dumbbell
(page 61)
2 sets, 20 reps

CHEST AND BACK

Superset (alternate sets) as follows:

Push-Ups, Standard
(page 76)
or
From the Knees
(page 75)
3 sets, 8 reps
(Short version:
2 sets, 8 reps)

superset with

Shrug
(page 74)
3 sets, 8 reps
(Short version:
2 sets, 8 reps)

Pullover
(page 80)
3 sets, 8 reps
(Short version:
2 sets, 8 reps)

If you have a bench and barbell, substitute
Bench Press
(page 78)
3 sets, 8 reps

superset with

Straight-Leg Dead Lift
(pages 69–70)
3 sets, 8 reps
(Short version:
2 sets, 8 reps)
Use a barbell if you have one.

Fly, variation
(page 79)
3 sets, 8 reps
(Short version:
2 sets, 8 reps)

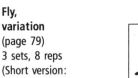
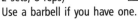

superset with

Upright Row
(page 73)
3 sets, 8 reps
(Short version:
2 sets, 8 reps)

ABDOMINALS

Optional on days 1 and 3. Your choice of 2 of the following exercises each workout, 1 set of as many as you can of each:
Half Sit-Up (page 103)
Tailbone Lift (page 106)
Abdominal Crunch — Center (page 101)
Ab Curl/Leg Lift (page 102) 20–40 reps

COOL-DOWN STRETCHES

Perform two stretches for each body part.

SUGGESTED WARM-UPS

Neck—**Turn** and **Nod** (page 25)
Shoulders and Arms—**Roll** and **Shrug** (page 26)
Chest and Back—**Arm Raise to the Rear** (page 27) and **Standing Arch-Curl** (page 28)
Torso—**Bent-Over Twist** (page 31) and **Side Bend** (page 30)
Lower Back—**Roll-Down** (page 31)
Ankles—**Roll** (page 35)
Calves—**Lift** (page 36)

SHOULDERS

Side Lateral, variation D
(page 83)
3 sets, 8 reps
(Short version: 2 sets, 8 reps)

Front Shoulder Raise, variation C
(page 84)
3 sets, 8 reps
(Short version: 2 sets, 8 reps)

Shoulder Press, variation D
(page 81)
3 sets, 8 reps
(Short version: 2 sets, 8 reps)

TRICEPS AND BICEPS

Superset (alternate sets) as follows:

Dip
(page 97)
3 sets, 8 reps
(Short version: 2 sets, 8 reps)

superset with

Preacher Curl
(page 91)
3 sets, 8 reps
(Short version: 2 sets, 8 reps)

Black Eye, variation
(page 96)
3 sets, 8 reps
(Short version: 2 sets, 8 reps)

superset with

Side Curl, variation B
(page 89)
3 sets, 8 reps
(Short version: 2 sets, 8 reps)

ABDOMINALS

Your choice of 2 of the following exercises each day, 1 set of as many as you can of each:
Half Sit-Up (page 103)
Tailbone Lift (page 106)
Abdominal Crunch—Center (page 101)
Ab Curl/Leg Lift (page 102) 20–40 reps

CALVES

Seated Calf Raise
(page 108)
1 set, 10 reps each position

FOREARMS AND WRISTS

Side Reverse Curl
(page 111)
1 set, 10 reps

Forward Wrist Curl
(page 112)
1 set, 10 reps
Use a barbell if you have one.

COOL-DOWN STRETCHES

Perform two stretches for each body part.

Programs Emphasizing Lower Body

The following programs are designed for people (especially women) who want to emphasize the legs, hips, and buttocks, but still get a complete workout. The first program (number 10) is a fairly easy, beginning- to intermediate-level program emphasizing the lower body. The second program (number 11) is for those who have been working out for a while already. It allows you to vary your program by picking your own exercises from the lists provided.

PROGRAM 10
(level two)

SUGGESTED WARM-UPS

Neck — **Nod** (page 25)
Shoulders and Arms — **Arm Swing** (page 26)
Chest and Back — **Standing Arch-Curl** (page 28)
Torso — **Twist** (page 29)
Lower Back — **Roll-Down** (page 31)
Legs — **Standing Leg Extension** (page 32) and **Dip** (page 33)
Hips — **Swing** (page 34) and **Side Lunge** (page 35)
Ankles — **Roll** (page 35)
Calves — **Lift** (page 36)

Note: Because this program emphasizes the lower body, take twice as much time as usual for each of the lower back, leg, and hip warm-up exercises.

LOWER BODY

Standing Exercises

Standard Squat
(pages 52–53)
3 sets of 8 reps
(Short version:
2 sets, 8 reps)
Use a barbell if you have one.

Side Lunge
(page 57)
3 sets, 8 reps
(Short version:
2 sets, 8 reps)

Stair Climbing
or **Step-Up**
(page 58)
3 sets, 8 reps
(Short version:
2 sets, 8 reps)

If you have home gym equipment, substitute
Seated Leg Extension
(page 65)
3 sets, 8 reps

Floor Exercises

Knee Lift to the Rear with Dumbbells
(page 61)
2 sets, 20 reps
(Short version:
1 set, 30 reps)

Double Leg Curl
(page 66)
2 sets, 10 reps
(Short version:
1 set, 15 reps)

If you're using home gym equipment, substitute
Hamstring Flexor
(page 66)
2 sets, 10 reps

ABDOMINALS

Center Curl-Up
(page 100)
as many reps as you can

Knee-Up
(page 105)
as many as you can

BACK

Bent-Over Row
(page 71)
3 sets, 8 reps
(Short version:
2 sets, 8 reps)

CHEST

Dumbbell Press
(page 77)
3 sets, 8 reps
(Short version:
2 sets, 8 reps)

SHOULDERS

Shoulder Press
(page 81)
3 sets, 8 reps
(Short version:
2 sets, 8 reps)
Use a barbell if you have one.

TRICEPS

Overhead Extension
(page 92)
3 sets, 8 reps
(Short version:
2 sets, 8 reps)

BICEPS

Regular Curl
(page 86)
3 sets, 8 reps
(Short version:
2 sets, 8 reps)
Use a barbell if you have one.

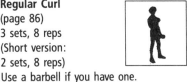

COOL-DOWN STRETCHES

Perform one stretch for each upper body part (neck, shoulders, back, etc.), and three lower body stretches of your choice.

PROGRAM 11
(level four)

This program is a little longer and more difficult than most of the programs in this book. It can be shortened as indicated.

SUGGESTED WARM-UPS

Neck — **Turn** (page 25)
Shoulders and Arms — **Shrug** (page 26)
Chest and Back — **Arm Raise to the Front** (page 27)
Torso — **Bent-Over Twist** (page 31)
Lower Back — **Roll-Down** (page 31)
Legs — **Standing Leg Extension** and **Dip** (page 32)
Hips — **Swing** (page 34) and **Side Lunge** (page 35)
Ankles — **Roll** (page 35)
Calves — **Lift** (page 36)

Note: Because this program emphasizes the lower body, take twice as much time as usual for each of the lower back, leg, and hip warm-up exercises.

LOWER BODY

Perform 2 or 3 standing legs and buttocks exercises (pages 52–58), 4 sets each exercise, 8 to 10 reps per set. (Short version: 2 exercises, 3 sets each) Perform 2 or 3 of the following floor exercises for legs and buttocks (pages 59–66), as indicated. (Short version: 1 or 2 exercises)

For **Fire Hydrants**, **Knee Lifts to the Rear**, **Pelvic Tilts**, and **Double Leg Curls**: 2 sets, 8 to 10 reps per set.

For **Inner Thigh Series**, **Quad Lifts**, and ⅔ **Side Leg Lifts**: 10 reps in each position.

For **Joy Kicks**: follow instructions in exercise description.

ABDOMINALS

Perform two abdominal exercises (pages 98–107), 1 set each exercise, as many reps as you can, or as instructed in description of exercise.

BACK

Choose two back exercises (pages 67–74). Perform 2 sets of 8 reps for each exercise. (Short version: 1 exercise, 2 sets)

CHEST

Choose two chest exercises (pages 75–80). Perform 2 sets of 8 reps for each exercise. (Short version: 1 exercise, 2 sets)

SHOULDERS

Choose two shoulder exercises (pages 81–85). Perform 2 sets of 8 reps for each exercise. (Short version: 1 exercise, 2 sets)

BICEPS

Choose one biceps exercise (pages 86–91). Perform 2 sets of 8 reps.

TRICEPS

Choose one triceps exercise (pages 92–97). Perform 2 sets of 8 reps.

CALVES

Choose one calf exercise (pages 108–109). Perform 1 set of 10 reps.

FOREARMS AND WRISTS

Choose one forearm or wrist exercise (pages 110–113). Perform 1 set of 10 reps.

COOL-DOWN STRETCHES

Perform one stretch for each upper-body part (neck, shoulders, back, etc.); and three lower-body stretches of your choice.

Programs Emphasizing Upper Body

The following programs are designed for people (especially men) who want to emphasize the upper body (chest, back, shoulders, and arms) but still get a complete workout. The first program below, number 12, is a beginning to intermediate Level Two program of medium duration. The following one, number 13, a Level Three program designed to build muscle mass, will take more time to perform. The third and fourth programs in this section, numbers 14 and 15, are Level Four — hard-core bodybuilding programs.

In addition to these programs, you can emphasize the upper body by taking any of the general programs for Levels One through Four, and skipping part (or all) of the leg exercises. Or, use the following programs as a pattern to design your own programs with different exercises, keeping in mind the basic principles discussed in chapter 2.

PROGRAM 12
(level two)

To be done 3 or 4 times per week.

SUGGESTED WARM-UPS

Neck — **Turn** and **Nod** (page 25)
Shoulders and Arms — **Roll**, **Shrug** and **Arm Swing** (page 26)
Chest and Back — **Arm Raise to the Front** and **Arm Raise to the Rear** (page 27)
Torso — **Twist** (page 29) and **Side Bend** (page 30)
Lower Back — **Roll-Down** (page 31)
Legs — **Dip** (page 33)
Hips — **Swing** (page 34)
Ankles — **Roll** (page 35)
Calves — **Lift** (page 36)

LOWER BODY

Standing Exercises

Standard Squat
(pages 52–53)
2 sets of 10
(Short version:
1 set, 10 reps)

Floor Exercises

Double Leg Curl
(page 66)
2 sets, 10 reps
(Short version:
1 set, 10 reps)

If you're using home gym equipment, substitute
Hamstring Flexor
(page 66)
2 sets, 10 reps

ABDOMINALS

Center Curl-Up
(page 100)
2 sets, as many reps as you can
(Short version: 1 set)

Leg Extension
(page 104)
2 sets, as many reps as you can
(Short version: 1 set)

BACK

Dead Lift
(pages 68–69)
3 sets, 10 reps
(Short version:
2 sets, 10 reps)

Bent-Over Row
(page 71)
3 sets, 10 reps
(Short version:
2 sets, 10 reps)

If you have home gym
equipment, add
Lat Pull-Down
(page 74)
3 sets, 10 reps

CHEST

Dumbbell Press
(page 77)
3 sets, 10 reps
(Short version:
2 sets, 10 reps)

Pullover
(page 80)
3 sets, 10 reps
(Short version:
2 sets, 10 reps)

SHOULDERS

**Shoulder Press,
variation D**
(page 81)
3 sets, 10 reps
(Short version:
2 sets, 10 reps)

**Front Shoulder Raise,
variation A**
(page 84)
3 sets, 10 reps
(Short version:
2 sets, 10 reps)

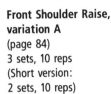

TRICEPS

Combination Kickback
(page 95)
3 sets, 10 reps
(Short version:
2 sets, 10 reps)

Dip
(page 97)
3 sets, 10 reps
(Short version:
2 sets, 10 reps)

BICEPS

**Hammer Curl,
variation C**
(page 88)
3 sets, 10 reps
(Short version:
2 sets, 10 reps)

Regular Curl
(page 86)
3 sets, 10 reps
(Short version:
2 sets, 10 reps)

CALVES

Standing Calf Raise
(page 109)
1 set, 15 reps

FOREARMS AND WRISTS

Reverse Curl
(page 110)
1 set, 15 reps

Forward Wrist Curl
(page 112)
1 set, 15 reps

COOL-DOWN STRETCHES

Perform two stretches for each upper
body part and one lower body stretch of
your choice.

Follow the guidelines to Level Three programs on page 128.

SUGGESTED WARM-UPS

Neck — **Turn** and **Nod** (page 25)
Shoulders and Arms — **Roll, Shrug** and **Arm Swing** (page 26)
Chest and Back — **Standing Arch-Curl** (page 28)
Torso — **Bent-Arm Twist** and **Turn-Out** (page 29)
Lower Back — **Roll-Down** (page 31)
Legs — **Standing Leg Extension** (page 32)
Hips — **Side Lunge** (page 35)
Ankles — **Roll** (page 35)
Calves — **Lift** (page 36)

LOWER BODY

Standing Exercises

Pole Squat
(page 55)
2 sets, 10 reps
(Short version:
1 set, 10 reps)

Floor Exercises

Quad Lift
(page 64)
2 sets, 10 reps
(Short version:
1 set, 10 reps)

If you have home gym equipment, substitute
Seated Leg Extension
(page 65)
2 sets, 10 reps

ABDOMINALS

Abdominal Crunch — Center
(page 101)
2 sets, as many as you can
(Short version: 1 set)

Knee-Up
(page 105)
2 sets, as many as you can
(Short version: 1 set)

CHEST

Fly
(page 79)
4 sets, 8 reps
(Short version:
3 sets, 8 reps)

Dumbbell Press
(page 77)
4 sets, 8 reps
(Short version:
3 sets, 8 reps)

If you have a bench and barbell, substitute
Bench Press
(page 78)
4 sets, 8 reps

Standard Push-Up
(page 76)
1 set, as many as you can
(Short version: 1 set)

BACK

Straight-Leg Dead Lift
(pages 69–70)
4 sets, 8 reps
(Short version:
3 sets, 8 reps)
Use a barbell if you have one.

Bent-Over Row
(page 71)
4 sets, 8 reps
(Short version:
3 sets, 8 reps)

Shrug
(page 74)
4 sets, 8 reps
(Short version:
3 sets, 8 reps)

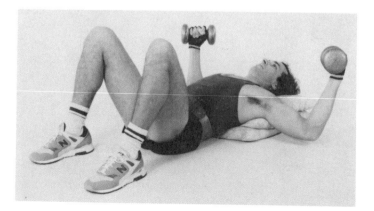

SUGGESTED WARM-UPS

Neck — **Turn** and **Nod** (page 25)
Shoulders and Arms — **Roll, Shrug**, and **Arm Swing** (page 26)
Chest and Back — **Standing Arch-Curl** (page 28)
Torso — **Bent-Arm Twist** (page 29) and **Turn-Out** (page 30)
Lower Back — **Roll-Down** (page 31)
Ankles — **Roll** (page 35)
Calves — **Lift** (page 36)

SHOULDERS

Side Lateral, variation A
(page 85)
4 sets, 8 reps
(Short version:
3 sets, 8 reps)

Arnold Press
(page 82)
4 sets, 8 reps
(Short version:
3 sets, 8 reps)

Reverse Fly
(page 85)
4 sets, 8 reps
(Short version:
3 sets, 8 reps)

BICEPS

Concentration Curl
(page 87)
4 sets, 8 reps
(Short version:
3 sets, 8 reps)

Preacher Curl
(page 91)
4 sets, 8 reps
(Short version:
3 sets, 8 reps)

Side Curl
(page 89)
4 sets, 8 reps
(Short version:
3 sets, 8 reps)

TRICEPS

Overhead Extension, variation
(page 92)
4 sets, 8 reps
(Short version:
3 sets, 8 reps)

Straight-Arm Kickback
(page 94)
4 sets, 8 reps
(Short version:
3 sets, 8 reps)

Dip
(page 97)
4 sets, 8 reps
(Short version:
3 sets, 8 reps)

ABDOMINALS

Half Sit-Up
(page 103)
2 sets, as many as you can
(Short version: 1 set)

Tailbone Lift
(page 106)
2 sets, as many as you can
(Short version: 1 set)

CALVES

Seated Calf Raise
(page 108)
1 set, 10 each position

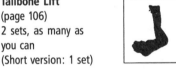

FOREARMS AND WRISTS

Side Reverse Curl
(page 111)
1 set, 15 reps

Reverse Wrist Curl
(page 113)
1 set, 15 reps

COOL-DOWN STRETCHES

Perform two stretches for each upper-body part and one lower-body stretch of your choice.

Follow the guidelines to Level Four programs on page 132.

This is a flexible program which can be done in its entirety, or split into two separate workouts. Below are two options on how to split up the program. Stick with the order of exercises given for each day so as not to violate the principle of starting with the largest muscles.

SPLIT OPTION 1

Days 1 & 3
Abdominals, lower body, chest, back, calves

Days 2 & 4
Abdominals, shoulders, triceps, biceps, forearms and wrists

SPLIT OPTION 2

Days 1 & 3
Abdominals, lower body, back, shoulders, biceps

Days 2 & 4
Abdominals, chest, triceps, forearms and wrists, calves

If you do the entire program in one session, three workouts per week is enough. With a split program, you should work out four to five times per week total. On the off days give your upper body a break and either do some aerobic exercise or rest.

SUGGESTED WARM-UPS

Neck — **Turn** and **Nod** (page 25)
Shoulders and Arms — **Roll**, **Shrug** and **Arm Swing** (page 26)
Chest and Back — **Standing Arch-Curl** (page 28)
Torso — **Bent-Arm Twist** (page 29) and **Turn-Out** (page 30)
Lower Back — **Roll-Down** (page 31)
Legs — **Standing Leg Extension** (page 32)
Hips — **Side Lunge** (page 35)
Ankles — **Roll** (page 35)
Calves — **Lift** (page 36)

ABDOMINALS

Twist
(page 98)
1 set, 50 reps
(25 each side)

Side Bend
(page 99)
1 set, 50 reps
(25 each side)

Ab Curl/Leg Lift
(page 102)
or
Side Curl-Up
(page 100)
2 sets, as many as you can
(Short version: 1 set)

LOWER BODY

Standing Exercises

Standard Squat
(pages 52–53)
2 sets, 8 reps
(Short version:
1 set, 8 reps)
Use a barbell if you have one.

Standard Lunge
(page 56)
2 sets, 8 reps
(Short version:
1 set, 8 reps)

Floor Exercises

Double Leg Curl
(page 66)
3 sets, 8 reps
(Short version:
2 sets, 8 reps)

If you're using home gym equipment, substitute
Hamstring Flexor
(page 66)
3 sets, 8 reps

BACK

Upright Row
(page 73)
4 sets, 6–8 reps
(Short version:
3 sets, 6–8 reps)

Good Morning
(page 67)
4 sets, 6–8 reps
(Short version:
3 sets, 6–8 reps)
Use a barbell if you have one.

Bent-Over Row, variation B
(page 71)
4 sets, 6–8 reps
(Short version:
3 sets, 6–8 reps)

CHEST

Dumbbell Press
(page 77)
4 sets, 6–8 reps
(Short version:
3 sets, 6–8 reps)

If you have a bench and barbell, substitute
Bench Press
(page 78)
4 sets, 6–8 reps

Fly
(page 79)
4 sets, 6–8 reps
(Short version:
3 sets, 6–8 reps)

Pullover
(page 80)
4 sets, 6–8 reps
(Short version:
3 sets, 6–8 reps)

SHOULDERS

**Shoulder Press,
variation C**
(page 81)
4 sets, 6–8 reps
(Short version:
3 sets, 6–8 reps)

**Front Shoulder Raise,
variation C**
(page 84)
4 sets, 6–8 reps
(Short version:
3 sets, 6–8 reps)

**Side Lateral,
variation D**
(page 83)
4 sets, 6–8 reps
(Short version:
3 sets, 6–8 reps)

TRICEPS

Black Eye
(page 96)
4 sets, 6–8 reps
(Short version:
3 sets, 6–8 reps)

Kickback
(page 93)
4 sets, 6–8 reps
(Short version:
3 sets, 6–8 reps)

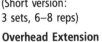

Overhead Extension
(page 93)
4 sets, 6–8 reps
(Short version:
3 sets, 6–8 reps)

BICEPS

**Regular Curl,
variation B**
(page 86)
4 sets, 6–8 reps
(Short version:
3 sets, 6–8 reps)

**Hammer Curl,
variation A**
(page 88)
4 sets, 6–8 reps
(Short version:
3 sets, 6–8 reps)

Side Curl
(page 89)
4 sets, 6–8 reps
(Short version:
3 sets, 6–8 reps)

CALVES

Standing Calf Raise
(page 109)
3 sets, 10 reps
(Short version:
2 sets, 10 reps)

FOREARMS AND WRISTS

Reverse Curl
(page 110)
2 sets, 10 reps
(Short version:
1 set, 10 reps)

Forward Wrist Curl
(page 112)
2 sets, 10 reps
(Short version:
1 set, 10 reps)

COOL-DOWN STRETCHES

Perform two stretches for each upper-body part and two lower-body stretches of your choice.

PROGRAM 15
(level four)

Follow the guidelines to Level Four programs on page 132.

You can do this program all in one session or split it as with the previous program. Since this program uses the technique of "pyramiding" (see formula here and page 149 for more information), it is time-consuming and very strenuous; most people will find it preferable to split the program into two workouts using the chart on page 142.

Since this workout emphasizes the upper body, the pyramiding formula should not be applied to the lower-body exercises. Also, there is no need to pyramid on abdominal exercises, forearm and wrist, and calf exercises.

Pyramiding Formula

1st set: Low weight, 10–12 reps
2nd set: Medium weight, 8 reps
3rd set: Highest weight, 2–5 reps
          (Use dumbbells heavy enough
          so that you are unable to do
          more than 5 reps.)
4th set: Low weight, 10–12 reps

SUGGESTED WARM-UPS

Neck—**Turn** and **Nod** (page 25)
Shoulders and Arms—**Roll**, **Shrug** and **Arm Swing** (page 26)
Chest and Back—**Arm Raise to Front**, **Arm Raise to Rear** (page 27) and

Standing Arch-Curl (page 28)
Torso—**Side Bend** (page 30) and **Bent-Over Twist** (page 31)
Lower Back—**Roll-Down** (page 31)
Legs—**Standing Leg Extension** (page 32)
Hips—**Swing** (page 34)
Ankles—**Roll** (page 35)
Calves—**Lift** (page 36)

ABDOMINALS

Two alternatives are listed for variety.

**Abdominal Crunch—
Center**
(page 101)
2 sets, as many as
you can
(Short version: 1 set)

Knee-Up
(page 105)
2 sets, as many as
you can
(Short version: 1 set)

or substitute

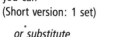

Leg Extension
(page 104)
2 sets, as many as
you can
(Short version: 1 set)

Side Curl-Up
(page 100)
1 set each side,
as many as you can

LOWER BODY

Standing Exercises

Standard Squat
(pages 52–53)
2 sets, 8 reps
(Short version:
1 set, 8 reps)

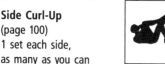

Standard Lunge
(page 56)
2 sets, 8 reps
(Short version:
1 set, 8 reps)

Floor Exercises

Quad Lift
(page 64)
3 sets, 8 reps
(Short version:
2 sets, 8 reps)

If you're using home gym
equipment, substitute
Seated Leg Extension
(page 65)
3 sets, 8 reps

BACK

Dead Lift
(pages 68–69)
4 sets, 8 reps
Use a barbell if you have one.

Note: Although some bodybuilders use
the pyramiding technique for all exercises, we do not recommend pyramiding
with exercises for the lower back, such
as the Dead Lift.

Upright Row
(page 73)
Use pyramiding
formula.

Bent-Over Row
(page 71)
Use pyramiding
formula.

CHEST

Dumbbell Press
(page 77)
Use pyramiding
formula.

If you have a bench and
barbell, substitute
Bench Press
(page 78)
Use pyramiding
formula.

Fly
(page 79)
Use pyramiding
formula.

Pullover
(page 80)
Use pyramiding
formula.

SHOULDERS

Shoulder Press
(page 81)
Use pyramiding
formula.
Use a barbell if you
have one.

Front Shoulder Raise
(page 84)
Use pyramiding
formula.

Side Lateral
(page 83)
Use pyramiding
formula.

TRICEPS

**Black Eye,
variation**
(page 96)
Use pyramiding
formula.

**Overhead Extension,
variation**
(page 92)
Use pyramiding
formula.

**Straight-Arm
Kickback**
(page 94)
Use pyramiding
formula.

BICEPS

Hammer Curl
(page 88)
Use pyramiding
formula.

**Side Curl,
variation B**
(page 89)
Use pyramiding
formula.

Preacher Curl
(page 91)
Use pyramiding
formula.

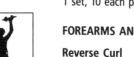

CALVES

Seated Calf Raise
(page 108)
1 set, 10 each position

FOREARMS AND WRISTS

Reverse Curl
(page 110)
2 sets, 10 reps
(Short version:
1 set, 10 reps)

Reverse Wrist Curl
(page 113)
2 sets, 10 reps
(Short version:
1 set, 10 reps)

COOL-DOWN STRETCHES

Perform two stretches for each upper-
body part and two lower-body stretches
of your choice.

Circuit Programs

The following Circuit Programs are designed for general fitness. In these programs, also known as "peripheral heart training," you do only one set of one exercise for each body part before moving on to the next body part. These programs will not change the shape of your body as effectively as the regular programs above. However, they do provide some strengthening and toning benefits, and if done with little resting between sets they will provide you with a minimal aerobic workout.

These are the quickest workouts, and are good for maintaining your strength and body tone on days when you can't make the time for a regular workout. The entire workout can be done once, twice, or three times through. These programs are a good choice for those who reserve most of their exercise time for another sport; they will enhance your abilities in that sport without taking too much time away from it.

PROGRAM 16
(circuit)

Twist
(page 98)
1 set, 50 reps

Center Curl-Up
(page 100)
1 set, as many as
you can

Standard Squat
(pages 52–53)
1 set, 10 reps

Joy Kick
(page 59)
1 set, as indicated in
description of exercise

**Bent-Over Row,
variation**
(page 71)
1 set, 10 reps

Dumbbell Press
(page 77)
1 set, 10 reps

**Shoulder Press,
variation C**
(page 81)
1 set, 10 reps

Kickback
(page 93)
1 set, 10 reps

Regular Curl
(page 110)
1 set, 10 reps

Standing Calf Raise
(page 109)
1 set, 10 reps

Forward Wrist Curl
(page 112)
1 set, 10 reps

If you have time, repeat program. Do entire sequence one to three times.

COOL-DOWN STRETCHES

Perform one stretch for each body part.

Side Bend
(page 99)
1 set, 50 reps

Abdominal Crunch—Center
(page 101)
1 set, as many as you can

Standard Lunge
(page 56)
1 set, 10 reps

Knee Lift to Rear with Dumbbell
(page 61)
1 set, 10 reps

Dead Lift
(pages 68–69)
1 set, 10 reps

Fly
(page 79)
1 set, 10 reps

Arnold Press
(page 82)
1 set, 10 reps

Overhead Extension
(page 92)
1 set, 10 reps

Concentration Curl
(page 87)
1 set, 10 reps

Seated Calf Raise
(page 108)
1 set, 10 reps

Side Reverse Curl
(page 111)
1 set, 10 reps

If you have time, repeat program. Do entire sequence one to three times.

COOL-DOWN STRETCHES

Perform one stretch for each body part.

It's easy to make up your own circuit programs. Just pick one exercise for each muscle group from the exercises in chapter 7. Do one set of ten repetitions of each exercise. For the abdominal exercise, follow instructions in the exercise description; usually they will tell you to do as many reps as you can.

Designing Your Own Program

Once you've worked with our programs for a while and have a feel for the basics of working out, you might like to create your own program, in order to add variety and to target specific areas of concentration. Here are some important principles to keep in mind when designing your own program:

1. Follow the general guidelines discussed in chapter 2 regarding reps and sets, correct order of exercises, and balance.

2. When designing your program, work at least two related muscle groups per session, in order to keep the oxygen flowing to that area of the body. Related muscle groups just means any two or more parts of the upper body, not including abdominals, (such as chest and back, chest and shoulders, triceps and biceps) or any two parts of the lower body (buttocks and thighs, thighs and calves, and so on).

3. In each workout session, perform at least two (preferably three) exercises per muscle group, and no more than four exercises per muscle group.

4. Do 3 or 4 sets of each exercise, 8 to 12 reps per set.

5. Work out each area of the body at least twice a week for best results. If you only have time for three workouts a week, do a whole-body workout each time.

6. As you become stronger, add more reps up to 12 reps per set. When you can do 3 or 4 sets of 12 reps of an exercise, it's time to increase the weight of the dumbbells you're using for that exercise. When you increase the weight, go back down to 8 reps.

7. Abdominals can (and should) be worked each training session, if you have time. Because abdominal muscles are not attached to any joints, they do not require as much rest as the other muscle groups. Balance your abdominal work, making sure that you do exercises for the upper, middle, and lower portions of the abs.

8. Be sure to incorporate rest time between sets into the total time allotted for each training session.

9. Remember that a workout log can be a powerful motivational tool and also make your workout more fun by allowing you to compete against your own past performance.

Joy Kicks are great for shaping your hips.

Workout Strategies for Different Goals

The basic guidelines above will help you create an all-purpose weight-training program that will strengthen, shape, and tone your body. If your goals are more ambitious or more modest than that, here is how to tailor a workout program to match specific goals, from the easiest up to the most demanding:

For general fitness and minimal strengthening benefits, with no real change in body shape, one exercise per body part and one set of about 12 reps per exercise. Don't go too heavy in weight for such a program, and try to keep your heart rate up by not resting any longer than you need to between exercises. (Even this kind of semi-aerobic "peripheral heart action" program should ideally be supplemented with some sustained aerobic exercise such as cycling, jogging, or swimming, or aerobics classes in order to achieve overall fitness.)

For toning and strengthening your muscles without substantially reshaping your body, do 12 to 15 reps per set. Of course, you will have to use somewhat lighter weights in order to do the extra repetitions. Do 3 or 4 sets per exercise as with the standard programs.

To shape, tone, and strengthen your body, follow the basic guidelines set out in the programs and in the discussion above on designing your own program. An ideal workout schedule would include 3 or 4 workouts a week, of 45 to 90 minutes per workout. Even if your program is toward the lower end of this range, you will start to see and feel the results within four weeks. But within this broad range, the person who devotes more time and energy to training will obtain quicker and more apparent results.

For adding substantial muscle size (bodybuilding), do fewer reps with heavier weights, and strive to reach muscle failure (the inability to do any more reps) by the time you do the last set of any exercise. Sets of 4 to 8 reps will be most effective for bodybuilding; increase the weight of your dumbbells accordingly. In general, if you want to add muscle bulk, you will need to devote

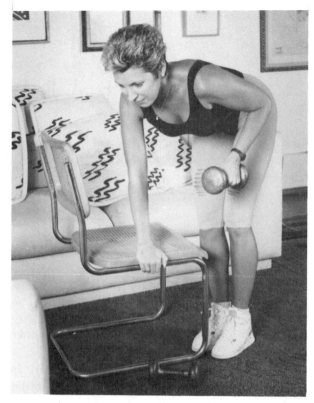

Dumbbells are great for toning . . .

. . . or for bodybuilding.

more time to weight training; plan on at least 4 sessions a week, 90 minutes per session. Even with this schedule, women need not worry about getting too large; the only way for most women to develop "manly" muscles is to work out with heavy weights several hours a day and/or take steroids (which have dangerous side effects and are *not recommended for anyone*).

As physical therapy to recover from an injury, with your doctor's approval always train the injured body part first (*after a warm-up*). You should train the injured part more frequently, too, preferably in every workout. Of course, don't work an injured area too hard at first—go lighter in weight and do more reps.

For any workout goal, one basic principle applies: the more often you train, and the longer each training session, the more rapid and dramatic your results will be.

Intermediate and Advanced Workout Techniques

The standard way of working out that we have described in this book is called the "straight-set method" (3 or 4 sets of each exercise, one exercise at a time, 3 to 4 exercises per body part, finishing one body part before moving on to the next). This is the most popular way to work out and is extremely effective. However, as you may have noticed in some of our intermediate and advanced programs in chapter 8, there are some alternative, equally effective methods. Here is a summary of the best intermediate and advanced methods, which you can incorporate into your own programs.

Supersetting means alternating sets of different exercises. The two exercises that you combine can be for the same muscle group or related muscle groups. For example, do one set of a dumbbell press for the chest, followed immediately by a set of one-arm rows for the back, then rest, and repeat the sequence until you have done 3 or 4 sets of each exercise. Or you can do a set of shoulder presses followed by a set of side laterals, another shoulder exercise. When supersetting within the same muscle group, choose two exercises that work different parts of the muscle. The benefits of supersetting are a more efficient, harder workout. You can rest one muscle group (or part of a muscle group) while you work another group (or another part of the same muscle group). Also, supersetting brings more oxygen to the area of your body that you're working.

Trisetting is the same as supersetting except that you do three exercises together instead of two. For example, a set of a shoulder exercise followed by a set of a biceps exercise followed by a set of a triceps exercise, repeating the sequence until you've done 3 or 4 sets of each. Or, you can triset within a single muscle group: a set of standard squats, a set of side lunges, and a set of joy kicks. (As with supersetting, choose exercises that work different parts of the same muscle.)

Pyramiding is recommended for those who have plenty of time for their workouts and whose primary goal is to add muscle mass. Start with numerous reps at a relatively low weight, then increase the weight with each set until you can only perform 2 to 5 reps. You can stop there and move on to your next exercise, or you can pyramid back down, either decreasing the weight with each set or dropping immediately down to your beginning weight. Allow yourself plenty of rest between sets, especially at the heavier weights.

Pyramiding Formula For the most popular pyramiding formula, do 4 sets of each exercise:

1st set:	Low weight, 10 to 12 reps
2nd set:	Medium weight, 8 reps
3rd set:	Highest weight, about 2 to 5 reps Use dumbbells heavy enough so that you are unable to do more than about 5 reps; do as many reps as you can.
4th set:	Low weight, 10 to 12 reps (same as the first set)

There is no need to pyramid on abdominal exercises, forearm and wrist, and calf exercises. Also, we do not recommend pyramiding on the lower-back exercises (Dead Lift, Straight-Leg Dead Lift, and Good Morning). Pyramiding requires you to lift heavier weights than any other style of working out, and a misjudgment could cause injury to the lower back, which is a "weak link" in many people. Also, if you have another area of the body, such as a shoulder, that has a chronic injury, it is best to avoid pyramiding on exercises for that muscle.

Specificity Training

If you have taken up weight training primarily to improve your skills in a particular sport, you will benefit from *specificity training*, that is, a weight-lifting program that emphasizes the muscles you use in your primary sport. If your sport is seasonal, these programs are also a great way to keep in shape during the off-season.

Specificity training programs are used by competitive athletes to improve their performance, and are not intended to provide a balanced workout. If you participate in a sport recreationally or for aerobic exercise, you may prefer to do just the opposite of specificity training, in order to exercise the muscles that are somewhat neglected by your primary sport. For example, runners and joggers may feel that their legs get plenty of exercise already, and they would be quite justified in choosing one of the workouts emphasizing the upper body.

Here are specificity programs for several popular sports.

Basketball & Volleyball

Back, Shoulders, Triceps: 3 or 4 exercises for each of these muscle groups every workout. Do 3 sets of each exercise.
Chest, Biceps: 1 exercise each, 3 sets.
Abdominals: 3 or 4 exercises.
Legs: Squat, Side Lunge, Front Lunge.
Stretching: Stretch every workout. Emphasize lower back.
Aerobic exercise: At least 3 times per week, 20 minutes or more.

Cycling

Legs: 3 or 4 exercises every workout, 3 sets each. Focus on standing exercises. Especially recommended: Step-Up.
Upper Body: 1 exercise, 3 sets, for each muscle group.

Abdominals: 3 exercises.
Stretching: Do not neglect stretching. Emphasize hamstrings, quadriceps, and lower back.

Running

Abdominals: 3 or 4 exercises.
Legs: Do Step-Up, 3 sets, and 2 floor exercises.
Chest, Back, Shoulders, Biceps, Triceps: 2 exercises each muscle group, 3 sets each exercise.
Stretching: Entire body. Emphasize hamstrings and lower back.

Soccer

Legs: 3 standing exercises, 3 sets each, and 2 floor exercises.
Abdominals: 3 exercises.
Back, Chest, Shoulders, Triceps, Biceps: 1 exercise each muscle group, 3 sets each exercise.
Stretching: Emphasize lower back and legs.
Aerobic exercise: 3 times per week or circuit program number 16 or 17, 3 times per week.

Swimming

Back, Shoulders, Triceps: 3 exercises each muscle group, 3 sets each exercise.
Abdominals: 3 exercises.
Legs: Lunge or Squat, 3 sets, and 3 floor exercises.
Chest, Biceps: 1 exercise each, 3 sets per exercise.
Stretching: Light stretching of entire body, emphasizing shoulders.
Circuit program: Number 16 or 17, 2 or 3 times per week.

Tennis

Abdominals: 5 exercises, including Twist and Side Bend.
Lower Back: Good Morning, plus either Dead Lift or Straight-Leg Dead Lift, 3 sets each exercise.
Legs: Lunge, Side Lunge, and Step-Up, 3 sets each.
Chest, Shoulders, Biceps, Triceps: 1 exercise each muscle group, 3 sets per exercise.
Forearms: Reverse Curl and Wrist Curl, 3 sets each.
Stretching: Entire body.
Aerobic exercise: 3 times per week.
Special: Stroke work with 5-pound dumbbell.

CHAPTER TEN

A Pep Talk

We all have times when we're tired, lazy, or just not in the mood to lift weights. Beginners are most susceptible to this condition. After a few consistent months on a program, however, you'll be amazed at how natural, pleasant, and satisfying weight training will feel.

So don't give up if the going is rough at first. Working out with weights is one of the smartest lifestyle choices you've ever made. It is an important part of your commitment to lifelong health, fitness, and vitality. Strength training will improve the quality of your life and allow you to feel more alive. This is the only body we get; there's no chance for a trade-in. By choosing to make it healthier and stronger, we increase our self-reliance, self-esteem, and enjoyment of life. Weight training is one of the most effective ways to slow down the aging process and to feel and look our best at all stages of our lives.

Have fun!

The authors (center, top and bottom) and three of their exercise demonstrators: Shelley Handley (right), Beverly Gannon (left), and Louis Williams (kneeling).

Muscle Chart

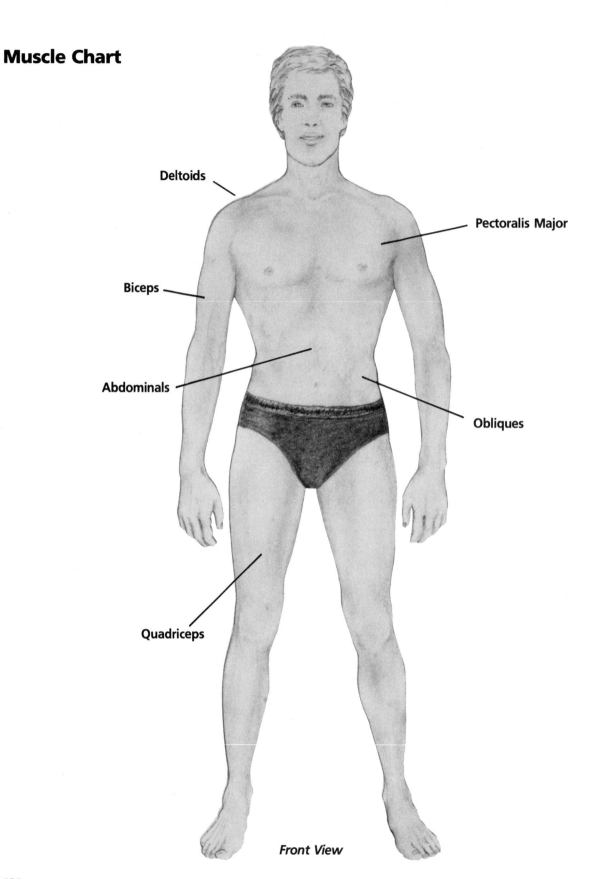

Deltoids

Pectoralis Major

Biceps

Abdominals

Obliques

Quadriceps

Front View

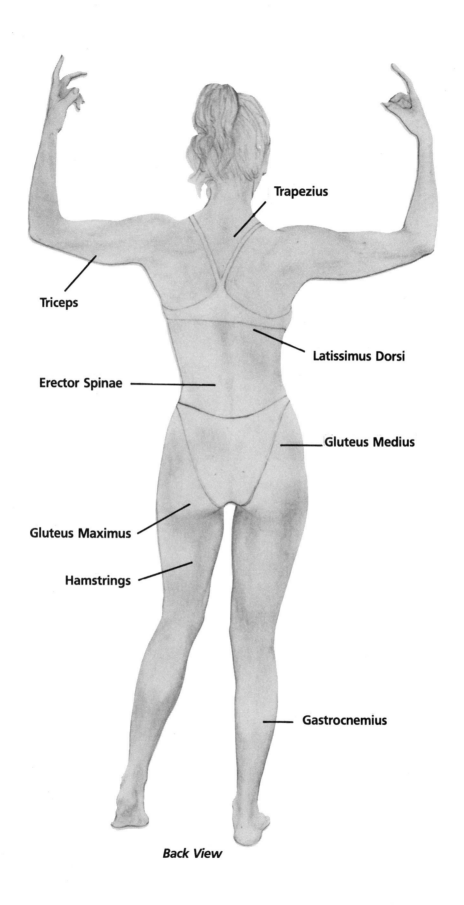

Trapezius

Triceps

Latissimus Dorsi

Erector Spinae

Gluteus Medius

Gluteus Maximus

Hamstrings

Gastrocnemius

Back View

Glossary

ABDOMINALS (ABS) The muscles that cover the front of the human body from just below the rib cage down to the hip bones.

AEROBIC FITNESS The body's capacity to efficiently deliver oxygen to the muscles so as to sustain vigorous exercise over a period of time.

AGILITY The capacity to change position and direction quickly, with precision and without loss of balance.

ALIGNED POSITION Standing with feet approximately parallel, shoulders and knees relaxed, pelvis tucked, and chin level.

ASSISTING MUSCLE A muscle that helps the main working muscle or body part to perform correctly.

BALANCE The principle of working opposing muscles evenly.

BARBELL A long weightlifting bar with removable plates, intended for use with both hands.

BICEPS The muscle in the front of the upper arm.

BODYBUILDING Subdivision of weight training in which the goal is to reshape the body and enhance muscle definition.

BODY COMPOSITION The ratio of body fat to lean body mass.

BODY PART Muscle group, such as chest, biceps, back, thighs.

BURN The sensation caused by products of fatigue that build up in the muscles as a result of vigorous exercise.

CALISTHENICS Exercises that use the weight of the body or parts of the body for resistance to increase muscular strength and endurance.

CARBOHYDRATES A primary foodstuff used for energy; carbohydrates are stored as glycogen and transported in the body as glucose.

CARDIOPULMONARY CONDITIONING Training that strengthens and improves the efficiency of the heart, blood vessels, and lungs, and leads to aerobic fitness. (*See* Aerobic Fitness)

CONNECTIVE TISSUE Ligaments and tendons, located in the joints, that bind together and support the various structures of the body.

DELTOIDS Shoulder muscles.

DUMBBELL Short-handled weightlifting bar with fixed or removable weights on each end, intended for use with one hand.

ERECTOR SPINAE The inner muscles of the lower back.

FLEXIBILITY Limberness of joints and muscles, measured by the ability to move joints through their full range of motion.

FREE WEIGHTS Barbells and dumbbells.

GASTROCNEMIUS The large calf muscle.

GLUTEUS MAXIMUS The large buttocks muscle.

GLUTEUS MEDIUS The rear upper-hip muscle.

HAMSTRINGS The large muscles in the backs of the thighs.

ISOLATION Focussing of weightlifting effort on one muscle or a part of a muscle.

LATISSIMUS DORSI (LATS) The primary and largest muscles of the back.

LIGAMENT The connective tissue that holds one bone to another.

MUSCLE FAILURE The state in which a muscle is completely fatigued and cannot perform even one more repetition of an exercise without first resting.

MUSCLE TONE The density (hardness) of a muscle.

MUSCULAR ENDURANCE Ability of a muscle or muscle group to exert force over an extended period of time.

MUSCULAR STRENGTH Degree of force that a muscle or muscle group can exert against a resistance.

OBLIQUES The muscles on either side of the abdominals; the waistline muscles.

OVERTRAINING Working out too much for too long without sufficient rest, which can decrease training effectiveness and lead to injuries.

PECTORALIS MAJOR (PECS) The large muscles of the chest.

PROPORTION (See Symmetry)

PROTEIN Compound made up of amino acids, which are responsible for building and repairing the body.

PULSE, PULSING A squeeze or tiny bounce that is sometimes added to the primary movement of an exercise.

PYRAMIDING A training method in which one performs an exercise with progressively heavier weights and fewer repetitions per set.

QUADRICEPS (QUADS) The large muscles in the front of the thigh.

RANGE OF MOTION (R.O.M.) The range within which a joint can move without hyperextension or hyperflexion.

REPETITIONS or REPS One complete movement of the weight or body part, through the full range of motion.

RICE Stands for Rest, Ice, Compression, and Elevation; a mnemonic code used for the proper treatment of injuries.

SET A group of repetitions performed without stopping or resting.

SPRAIN Overstretching or tearing of a ligament or of the synovial sac that cushions the joint.

STRAIN Overstretching or tearing of a muscle or tendon.

STRENGTH TRAINING Use of variable resistance (weightlifting) to build muscular strength and endurance.

SUPERSETTING Alternating back and forth between two exercises.

SYMMETRY Even development of the muscle groups in relation to each other and the body frame.

TENDON Connective tissue that holds muscle to bone.

TRAPEZIUS The muscle between the shoulders.

TRICEPS The muscle in the back of the upper arm.

TRISETTING Alternately performing sets of three different exercises.

VISUALIZATION Consciously programming the subconscious mind.

WARM-UP The first part of a workout; designed to prepare the body for vigorous exercise.

WEIGHT BELT Thick, strong belt used to support and protect the back while lifting weights.

WEIGHTLIFTING A form of exercise using variable resistance to strengthen, tone and shape the muscles and body.

WEIGHT TRAINING An exercise program based on weightlifting.

"WORKING THE NEGATIVE" Returning the weight to its starting position with a slow, controlled movement.

WORKOUT As used in this book, a weight training session.

Index

About the Authors

Stephenie Karony lives and works in Maui, Hawaii. She teaches exercise science and weight training at the Strong Stretched and Centered Body–Mind Institute. A personal trainer who has worked in the fitness field for thirteen years, she specializes in training clients in their own homes. Through that work she has pioneered new techniques, which are included in this book.

Stephenie Karony also designs individual programs and writes exercise prescriptions for clients at the Powerhouse Gym. She is certified by the American Council on Exercise as a personal trainer, and has certifications from several other national organizations. Her goal in writing this book, as in her other work, is to help people feel great about themselves.

Anthony Ranken also lives, works, and works out in Maui. His articles on a variety of topics have been published in several magazines and journals. He is a practising attorney and co-director of the non-profit organization Maui Tomorrow.